SCOTLAND'S TRADITIONAL HOUSES

FROM COTTAGE TO TOWER-HOUSE

Scotland's Historic Counties

0   10   20   30   40   50 Miles
0 10 20 30 40 50 60 70 80 Kilometres

Orkney

Shetland

WESTERN ISLES

Caithness

Sutherland

Ross and Cromarty

SKYE

Moray

Nairn

Banff

Aberdeen

Inverness

Kincardine

Angus

Perth

MULL

Argyll

Fife

Kinross

Clkmn

Stirling

Dumbarton

West Lothian

Midlothian

East Lothian

Renfrew

Lanark

Berwick

Bute

Peebles

Selkirk

Ayr

Roxburgh

Dumfries

Kirkcudbright

Wigtown

DISCOVERING HISTORIC SCOTLAND

SCOTLAND'S TRADITIONAL HOUSES

FROM COTTAGE TO TOWER-HOUSE

ELIZABETH BEATON

SERIES EDITOR: ALEXANDRA SHEPHERD

HISTORIC SCOTLAND

EDINBURGH: THE STATIONERY OFFICE

ABOUT THE AUTHOR

Elizabeth Beaton comes originally from Devon but has spent all her working life in Scotland. In the 1980s she was an Assistant Inspector for Historic Scotland in the Highlands and North-east: she is an active member of the Scottish Vernacular Buildings Working Group with a particular interest in rural and coastal buildings. She is the author of three volumes of the Royal Incorporation of Architects in Scotland series of illustrated guides : *Ross and Cromarty* (1992), *Sutherland* (1995) and *Caithness* (1996). She lives in Moray.

ACKNOWLEDGEMENTS

Special thanks to my helpful and ever-patient editor, Alexandra Shepherd, who contributed greatly to chapter two and to Margaret King, Angus Museums, and Veronica Steele, National Monuments Record, RCAHMS, who read and commented on the draft text besides helping with illustrations. Further assistance with illustrations from: Historic Scotland, particularly Jo White, Photo Librarian, Bernadette Goslin, Mark Watson and Pam Craig; National Trust for Scotland, Isla Robertson, Photo Librarian; Lyn Vesco, Angus Council; Andrew Miller, Clackmannanshire Council; Jane Thomas, National Monuments Record, RCAHMS. Also Nick Brown, Louise Crossman, Robin Falconer, Mike Finnie, Simon Montgomery, Joyce Rendall and George Tuckwell. Thanks to Gillian Kerr and George Bowie of The Stationery Office. Cover illustration: Front – corniced doorpiece, Banff, 1740 (Beaton); Muckrach Castle, Inverness-shire (Beaton) Back – cut-open reconstruction of Smailholm Tower (Historic Scotland); Crail, Fife (Beaton).

Published by The Stationery Office and available from:

The Stationery Office Bookshops

71 Lothian Road, Edinburgh EH3 9AZ (counter service only)

49 High Holborn, London WC1V 6HB
(counter service and fax orders only) Fax 0171-831 1326

68-69 Bull Street, Birmingham B4 6AD Tel 0121-236 9696 Fax 0121-236 9699

33 Wine Street, Bristol BS1 2BQ Tel 0117-926 4306 Fax 0117-929 4515

9-21 Princess Street, Manchester M60 8AS Tel 0161-834 7201 Fax 0161-833 0634

16 Arthur Street, Belfast BT1 4GD Tel 01232 238451 Fax 01232 235401

The Stationery Office Oriel Bookshop
The Friary, Cardiff CF1 4AA
Tel 01222 395548 Fax 01222 384347

The Stationery Office publications are also available from:

The Publications Centre (mail, telephone and fax orders only)

PO Box 276 London SW8 5DT
General enquiries 0171-873 0011
Telephone orders 0171-873 9090
Fax orders 0171-873 8200

Accredited Agents

(see Yellow Pages) and through good booksellers

© The Stationery Office 1997

First published 1997

ISBN 0 11 495785 1

British Library Cataloguing in
Publication Data

A catalogue record for this book
is available from the British Library

Applications for reproduction
should be made to
The Stationery Office Limited

CONTENTS

FOREWORD

Scotland is a country where the imprint of history is still clearly visible in the landscape, in its houses, churches, farmsteads and settlements large and small. All these have coloured, and been coloured by, their setting in mountains or moorland, on fertile pasture or sandy shore, at lochside or rivermouth. Of paramount importance has always been the all-encompassing influence of the sea, for Scotland is set amidst the sea roads of the Celtic provinces in the west and the Scandinavian regions of the north, the trading routes with the mainland of Europe to the east and the land and the sea approaches to that dominant neighbour, England, in the south. Scotland's cultural history has thus been moulded by a mixture of influences, fluctuating in importance, absorbed and transformed in ways that are peculiarly Scottish. This series aims to provide a view across the mosaic of that history from its earliest beginnings to the present day. Each volume covers one individual aspect of the panorama but the themes are interwoven: kings and queens, heraldry and houses, wars and warriors, stained glass and churches – all link to create a tapestry of Scotland's vigorous past and her historic present.

The great castles and grander houses of Scotland are well known to visitors but the more modest houses tend to be overlooked. Yet it is their character which does so much to stamp the landscape of country, town and coast with its distinctly Scottish flavour. This book seeks to show the whole range of these lesser-known dwellings from the very humble vernacular cottage to the more substantial homes of the small laird and rich merchant. It details those which still survive and surveys the history of their predecessors, following the varying strands in their development. It begins with a review of the materials used in construction which, together with details of shape and design, lend such a characteristicly Scottish essence to each of the buildings described.

ALEXANDRA SHEPHERD
Series Editor

INTRODUCTION

Scotland can boast the oldest standing house in Europe and a continuity of building traditions lasting well into this century. This vast timespan embraces a wide variety of homes – often the workplaces too – of farmers, merchants, crofters, fishermen, all types of artisans and their families.

Throughout this long development, change and continuity go hand in hand. The simple patterns of the 5,000-year-old stone dwellings still preserved on the Orkney islands, with their central hearths, box beds, stone shelves and cupboards, are repeated in varying forms down the centuries. The longhouse, in which man and beast share a single roof, was brought by the Vikings to their settlements in the north and west in the 9th century AD and continued in one form or another to be lived in until the middle of this century. The tall circular broch, a fortified farmhouse spanning

The home as the workplace: Johnnie Souter's (shoemaker) cottage, Kirkoswald (National Trust for Scotland).

Balmartine, Tiree: traditional cottages and houses of different types rubbing shoulders with one another. That to the left is in the Tiree vernacular, the other two can be found elsewhere in rural Scotland (Historic Scotland).

the years that mark the change from BC to AD, can be seen as the ancestor of the medieval defensive tower, and in turn of the domesticated tower-house, a vertical manor, entirely Scottish in character, that was the favoured home of merchants and landowners in the 16th and 17th centuries.

Developments in farming and fishing involved changing patterns of population: old settlements were abandoned, new ones established, often with home-based artisan work. Roads, canals and railways were constructed, requiring people – toll-keepers, lock-keepers, railmen – to live and work on these new arteries. Shepherds, keepers and stalkers were amongst those catered for in the characteristic cottages of the country estates. The expansion of textile manufacture and mining introduced industry to the countryside, again making for new workplaces, new settlements and renewed requirement for housing.

Colouring this long history of indigenous building is the skilled use of the assortment of local construction materials and the varied forms of the dwellings, adapted to suit the requirements and lifestyles of the occupants. These factors combined to produce a local vernacular, varying from region to region and from job to job. Such geographical variety defies easy classification, nor can there be neat chronological pigeon-holing for the small house, since often old types rubbed shoulders with the new, and buildings that were once rural, or at least in small burghs, have been surrounded and masked by later urban development.

This urban sprawl and the disappearance of some villages in large conurbations, combined with the appearance of the kit-house, identikit housing estates and the ubiquitous bungalow have served to blur recognition of many of these vernacular traditions. The great castles will always be visible but the more modest dwellings need greater perception to reveal their qualities. Yet

Fochabers, Moray where neat houses of around 1800 line the main street. The house in the centre was originally two dwellings with paired doorways, one now a window (Beaton).

in this long line of Scotland's secular building traditions, stretching from prehistory almost to the present day, we can find in coast and country a continuity and variation of vernacular housing as distinctive as any other national heritage. Moreover, these houses reveal more than simply building styles; they reflect the history of the occupants, their lifestyle and working practices; they are a palimpsest of people, mirroring a human saga.

Croft cottage, Sutherland (George Tuckwell).

CHAPTER 1

TRADITIONAL BUILDING MATERIALS

As an introduction to the richness of Scotland's vernacular architecture this chapter looks at the range of indigenous materials traditionally used in construction. These elements, together or singly, helped stamp local houses with their own regional individuality and contribute to the infinite variety of Scottish traditional homes.

OPPOSITE: *Fine drystone walling at the entrance to Dun Telve broch, 100 BC–AD 100 (Historic Scotland).*

Shetland Croft Museum, South Voe. The croft has a thatched ridge chimney (special to Shetland) and a round corn-drying kiln (Finnie).

Skilled drystone cottage walling, Kintail.
The varied boulders are infilled or 'cherry-caulked' (see opposite) with smaller fragments (Beaton).

Although stone is usually accepted as the typical traditional Scottish building fabric, a wide range of natural resources was exploited regionally as alternatives for walling where stone was not available or too costly to quarry and transport. Turf, clay, mud, wood, wattle, straw and other vegetable materials all played their part in traditional construction. As transport improved, slate became common for roofing, though pantiles enjoyed, and still enjoy, popularity in certain areas. Thatch was common well into the 20th century in both town and country. In an age of the ubiquitous kit house, standardised materials and DIY, these traditional variations lend colour and interest to the built landscape. As Alec Clifton-Taylor (1972, 10), a pioneer observer of the vital role of local building fabrics, put it: 'What matters to me, and I hope to my readers, is the visual aspect of our buildings, and the reason why they look as they do in one place, and perhaps so different only a few miles away.'

STONE

Stone, in all its geological variety, colour, texture, shape and size, is the most durable building material in Scotland. It is hard to win, heavy, sometimes bulky and often difficult to transport, yet it has been worked by generations of stonemasons, from prehistoric people with comparatively unsophisticated tools constructing homes in Orkney more than 5,000 years ago to the 17th-century Aberdeenshire Bel and Leiper families of master masons creating their exotic manorial tower-houses. Throughout, it has been used by those nameless skilled men who worked on the neat stone cottages and farmhouses which form such an important element in the rural landscape.

The contribution of the **quarriers** also should not be forgotten, for they knew the resources available and how to exploit them. Again, as Alec Clifton-Taylor put it:

'Stone is a miracle of nature. No two quarries are alike and all stones vary within the same quarry. The correct selection taxes the skill of the quarryman. A quarry is like a book written in a strange language: it must be studied to be understood'.

Scotland's stone is as visually varied as her landscape, displaying differing colours and textures besides different structural qualities. Granite is pink, yellow and all shades of grey; sandstone ranges from deep red to the palest cream, sometimes striated with contrasting hues; there is dark *greywacke* (grey and usually known as whinstone).

In Orkney and Caithness the flagstone splits easily into thin sections, a distinctive and fine material for neat dry-stone walling besides being exploited as lintels, stair treads, partitions and shelves.

While the finest sandstone *ashlar* (stone that has been tooled and polished to produce a smooth surface) was used on medieval prestigious work, mainly churches and castles, from the 17th century onwards it came into use for frontages and as margins around door and window openings, skewputts, crowsteps and other features. Polished ashlar is laid with the narrowest and finest mortar courses, producing barely visible straight lines. Where, however, good ashlar was not available but a near approximation sought, dressed blocks of stone sometimes have their slight irregularities levelled by the insertion of scraps of slate or pebble into the mortar courses, a practice known as *cherry-pointing*.

A more rough-and-ready form of masonry was universally produced from the random **rubble** gathered from the fields. Stones of all shapes and sizes were used to create continuous level masonry courses, with smaller stones and fragments used to level and as infill (*cherry-caulking*).

Where funds and materials were available, the frontage of a better class house could be of

Where it was difficult to cut stone, particularly granite, into neat shapes, the rough areas between vertical joints could be filled or **pinned** *with squares of small, contrasting stones making a virtue out of a necessity. This is common in north-east Scotland, from where the practice gets its name of 'Aberdeen bonding'. The contrast of dark and light grey, or pale grey and pink or red, is distinctive and gives added interest to an otherwise plain facade (Beaton).*

Chequered red and yellow tooled Ben Rinnes granite frontage, c.1795, Archiestown, Moray (Beaton).

dressed stone, cut square and tooled to produce a smooth surface. The return gables and rear would be of less expensive rubble, sometimes coated with harling, a mix of lime, grit and water which was cast over the surface to provide a protective coat.

Where good, easily-split sandstone and flagstone were available, such as Moray and Caithness respectively, stone sections were aligned to give a smooth return to the window and door openings, making vertical facing margins unnecessary. Where this type of stone was not available and dressed ashlar margins too expensive, then the rubble courses butted the window and door voids as best could be managed while the rubble walls were rounded at the corners. Similarly, adequate foundations could be constructed using random boulders, probably removed during preparation of ground for crops, as a footing: these are often substantial and project as a rough base course.

TURF

Turf is a ubiquitous material with a long ancestry of use either on its own or layered with stone. Turf used on its own for walling was discouraged by improving landlords in the 18th and early 19th centuries for it consumed topsoil and grass pasture. Alternate layers of flagstone and turf were identified at the Viking settlements at **Birsay** on Orkney and **Underhoull** and **Jarlshof**, both on Shetland, from about ad 900. At Todlochy, Monymusk, 'six or eight old-fashioned low-browed huts...built of turf and rough hill stones in alternate layers, the roofs...thatched with straw and roped diagonally after the manner of a hay stack', were described by Robert Thomson, a Nairnshire schoolmaster, as the homes of the cottars on his father's Aberdeenshire farm at the turn of the 1800s.

Glazed tomato house with turf walling, Island of Eigg, 1983. Layered turf is a living mass, valuable for its thermal and wind-resistant qualities. Though obsolete for dwellings, the skills and tradition were still active in the 1980s (Beaton).

Walling constructed from layers of turf and stones, (gathered from field clearance) sandwiched together, was common for both temporary dwellings and for the houses of cottars and day labourers. As late as 1816, new houses were being built of turf and stone on the island of Arran – sometimes as a co-operative effort for a newly married couple. The technique was found in the Borders, north-east and south-west Scotland and in the Highlands in Ross-shire and Caithness. The walls were not strong enough to be fully load-bearing, the roof of turf and thatch carried by pairs of *crucks* or *couples*, supporting roofing timbers, covered with sods and usually a top layer of thatch. There would be no ceiling: miscellaneous articles and foodstuffs, such as dried fish, were stored hanging from the roof timbers.

Dry turf is not fire resistant, so the hearth in these dwellings was always positioned in the centre, the smoke seeping out through the roof or through a central chimney stack. A hearth against a gable wall is only possible if that wall is stone or clay. These *creel-houses* were the usual type of dwelling in the northern and western Highlands until the mid-18th century and later. Although the predominant housing type for the poor, larger versions were homes to ministers, farmers, lairds and others of middle-range prosperity. In the mid-19th century, the 'curious Celtic mansion of Macdonnell of Glengarry', a creel house built a century earlier, was noted at Inverie in Knoydart, on the shores of Loch Nevis.

Scallop-shaped turf divots as underlay for thatching, Broubster, Caithness. The cottage was occupied until the 1960s (Beaton).

CLAY

Turf is an obsolete walling fabric now but **clay** is not, though *mud*masons (as distinguished from *stone*masons) have disappeared. Where stone is not abundant or has to be brought from a distance, clay or mud has long been exploited for building in Britain and elsewhere, notably in the Middle and Far East. Indeed the history of its use in building in Britain again goes back to prehistoric times: it was used for the foundations and sealing of walls more than 5,000 years ago in the Neolithic houses of Skara Brae on Orkney. Insulation is excellent, against both cold and heat. Socially, clay

Clay and bool revealed (Beaton).

*A local variant of clay construction is **clay and bool** or Auchinhalrig work, centred on the lower reaches of the River Spey in Moray and named after a hamlet there. Bools or rounded stones from the river are mixed with clay and chopped vegetation. In time some of the exterior clay wears away, giving the walling a nubbly appearance. As with pure clay, the walls were lime washed annually to protect them from damp. In Urquhart, Moray, this was part of 'spring cleaning'. If cared for, clay walls will last for many decades, even centuries.*

houses range widely: churches, cottages, farm steadings besides two-storey town houses. In 1624 the manse of King Edward parish, Aberdeenshire, was a two-roomed clay house. The areas where clay was used for building are in Speyside, east Sutherland, the northern and southern shores of the Moray Firth, parts of Aberdeenshire, Angus and the Solway Firth. Documentary evidence goes back at least to the 16th century: in 1586 there was a dispute in Forres in Moray over the ownership of mud-holes.

Clay was mixed with sand and vegetation, such as chopped grass, heather or straw, to a smooth solid consistency. Walls were constructed up to 0.61 m (2 ft) thick, starting at one corner of the house and working right round to where the mason had commenced. Ideally this last section would be dry and ready for the next course; work would then proceed until the desired height had been achieved. They were strong enough to support the roof: the only stonework was that used in corners, door and window lintels and foundations.

The sticky, malleable consistency of clay, drying firm and hard, lends itself to many uses. Interior walls were constructed of a **wattle** framework coated with mud. The framework would have been of available local materials, thin and pliable types such as hazel or willow. Frames were also made of upright stakes with horizontal lathes over which strands of straw were folded, hanging like fresh noodles put out to dry: this was plastered with clay to form a strong partition. A network of plaited straw or grass, stretched and coated with clay also served as party walling. Messy though it may seem (and undoubtedly was during construction!) this type of internal walling was not considered too humble a fabric for prestigious 17th-century tower-houses nor for fashionably symmetrical mansions. **Castle Fraser**, Aberdeenshire (completed 1636), has party walling in the attics of the plaited type while imposing 18th-century **Foulis Castle**, Ross-shire, has wattle-and-daub walls in ground-floor rooms.

The various combinations of clay and wattle rejoice in many local names, *cat and clay*, *clay and dab*, *stud and mud*, to name but a few.

Beaten, compacted and dried, clay made a good floor. One method of hardening the surface was to shut sheep into the house overnight. It was said that the combination of their droppings and persistent trampling made a wonderful surface which could be polished and be the pride of any housewife!

Brick gable, chimneys and skews, Old Aberdeen, where the Seaton Pottery, Brick and Tile Works was a local source (Shepherd).

BRICK

Brick is a product of the industrialisation of clay. The raw material was extracted from clay deposits, shaped in a mould, dried and then fired, producing a regular, easily handled and transported building material. Firing could be in field clamps on site or in specialised premises. **Brickworks** were established where the raw material and the demand were available. For example, in the north-east there were several brickworks, notably Craigellachie, Whitehills, Turriff and Cruden Bay: primarily these produced *land drains* (clay pipes used for field drainage) and pantiles. The excellent insulating properties of brick led to its use for lining garden walls, conserving warmth for ripening fruit and, conversely, lining the ice-houses associated with estuarine salmon fishing industry to retain the cold. Both these uses are of 19th-century origin. However, there were earlier brickworks at Seaton,

Glass

Early Scottish glass manufacture was confined to flint glass (for domestic ware) and bottle glass; window glass was probably imported into Scotland from northern England or the continent. This was spun or crown glass, the hot, molten metal spun until centrifugal force created a flat disc of brilliant glass from which small sections were cut and set as diamond-shaped panes in a fine lead framework. These glazed panels were fitted in upper casements in prosperous tower and merchant houses, the lower portion closed with wooden shutters. In 18th-century Scotland, the multi-pane sash-and-case window found universal favour in the contemporary symmetrical frontage. Bigger panes were achieved by later methods of glass production, particularly plate glass when the hot metal was rolled into large sheets and polished.

Aberdeen, and evidence of 17th–19th-century use of this material in the High Street, **Old Aberdeen**, where some houses have *brick tumbling*, ornamental and practical gable triangles where the brick is laid at right angles to the slope of the roof to provide a smooth base for the coping or skew, a 17th- and 18th-century practice common in the eastern counties of England from Kent to Lincolnshire.

The greatest concentration of Scottish brickworks was in the central belt, for fireclay was a by-product of the coal mining industry, much of the clay appearing as colliery waste in the *bings* (waste heaps). A substantial proportion of industrial housing in central Scotland is brick built, including that associated with the coal mines (see Chapter 7). The railway carried brick to unexpected places – railway linesmen's bothies usually have brick chimney stacks, whatever the walling. Once the problem of transport was solved, brick, with good insulating properties and regular shape, was exploited in unexpected locations where there had been no previous use.

WOOD

Although Scotland does not have a tradition of wooden Scandinavian-style houses, **wood** has always played an important part in construction and furnishing. An extraordinary and comparatively modern Scottish wooden-walled building tradition developed around Kingussie and Newtonmore, Inverness-shire, in the 1920s and 1930s, where reused railway sleepers were butted together vertically as walling. The basic building material of these dwellings is sometimes difficult to recognise as many have been harled.

Creel-houses with their turf-covered wooden framework have already been mentioned. In rural upland areas these predated the rubble stone cottages which we take for granted as an age-old vernacular type. The vital support element in these dwellings and others of similar construction was the series of cruck frames or *couples*, structural wooden arches not unlike the wishbone of a chicken. In small, humble houses these could be low arches: where there was a natural shortage of wood (Caithness and north Sutherland), the cruck trusses were made of reused material or branches twisted together, while more substantial timbers were required for larger houses.

Substantial timbers were needed for roofing in better class houses. From the 16th to the 18th century these were secured to the wall-head as triangular braces, the base of the triangle the *sole piece* and the vertical stay wedged against the inner side of the wall the *ashlar post*.

Large timbers were also used as **draw-bars**: a heavy wooden beam drawn from a mural cavity across a door to secure it. The *draw-bar hole* is often to be seen behind a door in larger mansions and is even visible in surviving prehistoric settlements such as Skara Brae on Orkney; the survival of the draw-bar itself is rarer.

Entwined timber cruck trusses seen at Laidhay Barn, Caithness. In houses these are usually hidden by later inserted ceilings. (Beaton).

Obviously house carpentry depends on the resources available, from the simplest wooden frames for box beds and basic furnishings in the poorer house to panelled walls, doors and window shutters and fine turned stair balusters in more prosperous housing where generous local supplies and skills were available. The range of timber employed varied according to local availability and means, **oak** being the preferred wood where possible. In Speyside, Inverness-shire and Moray, the extensive pine forests were a source of considerable wealth: internal house carpentry of dwelling houses associated with the estates, and the homes of better off farmers, factors and ministers were of fine workmanship.

Fine early 19th-century pine-panelled door, Strathspey (Beaton).

SLATE

Slate is clay or mudstone metamorphosed by intense pressure into a hard stone with regular close-set lines of cleavage, facilitating splitting into thin slabs and ideal for roofing. Some local sources were recognised quite early, such as at **Luss** in Dunbartonshire and **Aberfoyle**, Perthshire, from where, perhaps, the slates were transported to Doune Castle in 1581. Fragments of local slate remain embedded in the wallhead of roofless Blairfindy Castle, Glenlivet (1586), similar to those from the **Cnoc Fergan** surface quarries in neighbouring Strath Avon.

Slate quarriers' cottages, Easdale, Argyll. Piles of slate lie under the tree in the centre (Historic Scotland).

The Argyll quarries at **Easdale**, **Seil** and **Ballachulish** were of national importance. Much of the Easdale slate was below sea level: until the 1730s slates were quarried above the shoreline, after which a company was formed and various measures taken to drain off water, including pumps and a windmill. Production rose from 500,000 slates in 1745 to seven million in the mid-19th century! Slates were sent to Edinburgh by sea via Cape Wrath and there was important trade with Glasgow. Ballachulish was even more productive: in the mid-19th century the quarries were producing an incredible 15 million slates annually. One hundred and fifty years later, the quarries are closed but west coast slates are still in use and being reused.

There were quarries on the Banffshire–Aberdeenshire borders at **Foudland**, **Culsamond** and **Gartly**. These were surface quarries on exposed hillsides, far from the sea with its easier, cheaper marine transport. The construction of the Aberdeen–Inverurie canal in 1805 was a welcome boost and the quarries produced a million slates a year for the expanding city of Aberdeen. The market shrank with the coming of the railway from 1858 bringing cheaper, lighter Welsh slate and effectively reducing the demand for the heavier local product.

In the Elgin area, the easily split sandstone slabs were used as a heavy stone slate fixed with wooden pegs. Better known are the Caithness **flagstone** roofing slabs from quarries in the north of the county, producing both roofing slates and and flagstones for paving, besides a multiplicity of uses. Rich brown Caithness roofs, the slabs laid in diminishing courses, are a visual delight. As early as 1536 these stone slates were sent to Leith for roofing the chapel at Holyrood and in the 1640s 'twantie two thowsand skleatts' to Moray for Sir Robert Innes's new mansion house near Elgin. The slaters were paid for 'theaking [thatching] my houss', the verb synonymous with slating.

In some parts of Orkney very large slabs were laid on the low, single-storey cottages. These did not completely cover the roof nor fit comfortably, the gaps infilled with thatch.

THATCH

I can theik [thatch] wi auld rushes, wi heath o ling
Bent, bracken o docken o wi any wan thing

Thatch, with a variety of materials and techniques, was general throughout Scotland, in both town and country. As housing standards rose and as transport improved, this roofing tended to be concentrated in the country – it had long been recognised as a fire risk in congested urban areas.

Reed thatch, as practised in the Carse of Gowrie, Angus, had a long life. **Heather** too was strong and durable but involved much hard work pulling it from the hillsides and carrying it back to the location where it was to be used. Even where a less hardy material was employed, a heather fringe at eaves level threw off the surplus rainwater from the wallface. *Bent* (sea grass), *whins* (broom), bracken and rushes were all exploited. These were usually thatched over a turf base, the turfs laid on the roof timbers grass side downward, surviving many re-thatchings. The thatched roof was usually strengthened by a network of *simmons*, ropes twisted from grass or straw, crisscrossed over the thatch and held in place at the gable by wooden pegs. On the west coast, in Lochaber and parts of Inverness-shire, the thatch was retained by parallel rows of wands, mainly hazel, pinned in place with the same material. In the Western Isles and Skye the base of the thatch was anchored by a fringe of stone weights, while in Caithness long, narrow pieces of flagstone, *benlin stanes*, were slung the length

Rushes, cut and prepared for thatching, Caithness 1996 (Beaton).

Barrapol, Clachan Dubh, Tiree. Traditional building techniques adapting innovatory materials. The thatch is held down at the eaves with bricks rather than the usual rounded stones, the chimney stacks have industrial pottery chimney cans while the rear extension has a corrugated-iron roof. All these materials have been brought into Tiree (Historic Scotland).

of the roof where the thatch overhung the wallhead; at Ardersier, Inverness-shire, on the Moray Firth, a series of looped chains secured the clay thatch against stormy weather. Where thatch exists now, mainly on outbuildings, ubiquitous meshed chicken wire serves this purpose.

Depending on the material, thatching could last as much as a generation or as little as two years before needing to be replaced. Heather thatch put in place by a grandfather could survive for his grandchildren to admire; reed thatch might endure for 20 or 30 years but less sturdy forms such as bent grass would require replacement every other year.

Principally in the north-east, but coexistent with the clay building tradition (except Galloway), **clay thatch** was a roofing practice. Bunches of straw were inserted into a turf base and washed over with a clay slurry: repairs were effected by simply filling the gap with more clay and thatch. At least one farmer in Moray grew rye specially for thatching the farmworkers' cottages in the 1920s and 1930s.

CORRUGATED IRON

Though scarcely vernacular, **corrugated iron** or *crinkly tin* has created a tradition of its own as a building fabric. It was invented in London in 1828 by Henry Robinson Palmer (1795–1844); five years later John Claudius Loudon advocated the use of this material for a number of purposes in his *Encyclopaedia of Cottage, Farm and Villa Architecture*. Its use was not restricted to roofing or simple sheds. Corrugated-iron buildings were shown at the Great Exhibition in

London, 1851, where Prince Albert approved of them sufficiently to order a ballroom for Balmoral, amazingly erected within three weeks and still sound. During the second half of the 19th century, corrugated iron had become popular in Scotland, manufactured as kit buildings; they were wood-lined and kept warm and dry.

PANTILES

Pantiled roof with slate 'easing course' Cullen, Banffshire (Beaton).

The distinctive curved **pantiles** were produced in the industrialised brick and tile works which exploited local deposits of clay; they were not used commonly until after the 1850s. As a roofing material, they fell between slate and thatch in price, less expensive than slate but more costly – though also longer lasting – than most thatch. They are particularly associated with the Moray and Banffshire fishertowns and with the Lothians where there were substantial clay deposits connected with coal mines. Some, especially those manufactured in the north-east, were slightly porous and were occasionally treated with a tar slurry in coastal locations (pitch was used by the fishermen for various waterproofing tasks) to combat the incessant battering by gales, rain and sea spray: inland they could be covered with a layer of turf. The first few rows of a pantiled roof, the **easing course**, are often of more costly slate, covering the vulnerable wallhead and giving additional protection against both wind and rain. The cheerful warm red of a pantiled roof adds colour and vitality to groups of otherwise simple cottages, in the agricultural Lothians contrasting with the rich green and gold of the landscape. In the East Neuk of Fife and around St Andrews there is a silvery/brown/grey pantile, an unusual blend of colour and texture creating a distinctive and distinguished roof.

The variations in the types, use and treatment of stone within Scotland besides the exploitation of other indigenous materials, turf, clay, brick, wood and even corrugated iron, make observation of building fabric an ever fascinating ploy. The use of these diverse vernacular fabrics influences many Scottish building traditions, both geographically and chronologically, as we shall see in subsequent chapters.

CHAPTER 2

SCOTLAND BC AND LATER

EARLY HOMES AND VILLAGES

W e have surveyed the range of buildings that cover the Scottish landscape through the materials that were used to construct and furnish them. This chapter goes back to the beginning to look at the earliest houses in that tradition.

First in the northern isles of Orkney and Shetland and subsequently on mainland Scotland, archaeologists have identified examples of buildings and their indigenous materials which link, albeit with gaps, the development of the house and home from prehistory to our present vernacular. The surviving building material is predominantly stone, that most durable of construction fabrics, but there is evidence for the use of wood and for timber houses as far back as the early farming period, more than 5,000 years ago.

OPPOSITE: *Skara Brae – House 7 with the hearth, dresser and bed place to the right (Historic Scotland).*

Early houses at Knap of Howar, Papa Westray, Orkney (Historic Scotland).

THE EARLIEST HOUSES

It is exciting that the oldest standing man-made dwelling in Europe is in Scotland, at **Knap of Howar** on the northern Orkney island of Papa Westray. Bones from the food debris of the settlement have been scientifically dated and mean that the houses could have been built as early as 3600 BC. The site consists of two interconnecting buildings, roughly rectangular in shape with rounded corners. Each has its own paved entranceway, but a short passage through the thickness of the walls links the two. One house, slightly larger than the other, was divided into two rooms; the smaller, which may have acted as a workshop, was partitioned into three. The buildings are constructed from the local flagstone with fine dry-stone, double-skinned walls packed with midden to insulate and consolidate them; the flagstone splits easily to provide the large upright slabs which are used to make the room dividers and edge the entrances and connecting passage.

One of the houses retains its stone hearth in the central chamber of the living quarters; small alcoves, built into the walls, served as cupboards and the remains of stone benches or platforms can be seen along the walls. Timber would have been used for additional partitioning and as benches, and for the framework of the roof, the rafters resting on the tops of the corbelled walls, just as we shall see in the *blackhouses* (the traditional single-storey double-walled house) of the Western Isles. Quernstones used for grinding grain, pottery, bone and stone tools and midden debris combine to present a picture of a small farming community thriving beside the Orkney shore many centuries ago.

An even more remarkable survival is the unparalleled collection of houses making up the village of **Skara Brae** on the shores of the Bay of Skaill on the Orkney Mainland. This settlement of at least eight houses was built and re-built over a period of more than 600 years spanning the centuries around 3000 BC. Some of the houses stand to eaves level and their intercommunicating passages are still intact. Like Knap of Howar, the houses have thick, double-skinned walls, but they are somewhat different in plan, more square, with single, undivided living compartments. Their internal furnishings, constructed of the fine Orkney sandstone, are splendidly preserved and give a snap-shot of the well-appointed house of more than 4,000 years ago: there is a central hearth, flanked by beds on either side, and on the wall opposite the entrance a grand two-tier dresser. Cupboards, alcoves and small round cells were set into the walls, the latter possibly used for latrines, as the sophisticated drainage system

suggests. In the earliest houses the bedplaces were set into the thickness of the wall; later they were boxed into the floor space. The dressers are very striking: they anticipate and are similar to *court cupboards*, carved, inlaid and partially open-shelved wooden cupboards fashionable in the 17th-century on which household wares were displayed or stored in prosperous homes. Like the box beds and the central hearth, they also reflect the traditional furnishing of the vernacular Highland cottage: in essence, domestic patterns of hearth, beds and dressers remained little changed.

House 1 at Skara Brae with the bay in the background (Historic Scotland).

These early Orkney dwellings are exceptional in their antiquity and the details of their preservation. We are not so lucky with other Neolithic buildings which were not primarily constructed of stone nor preserved as these were beneath a blanket of sand. However at **Balbridie** in Aberdeenshire, on the banks of the river Dee, the timber postholes and *bedding trenches* of an even older, very impressive dwelling did survive, broadening our picture of the range of houses which would have studded the early landscape. This great timber hall, inhabited around 3500 BC, measured a massive 24 m long by 13 m broad, much like the great Neolithic timber longhouses of central Europe from where its ancestors are likely to have come. The roof

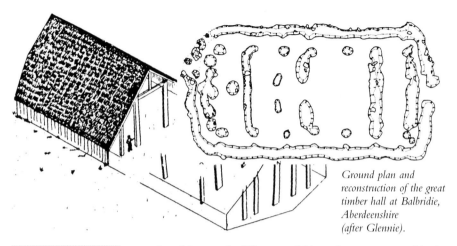

Ground plan and reconstruction of the great timber hall at Balbridie, Aberdeenshire (after Glennie).

The Ring-Ditch House

This type of round-house, found in southern Scotland, is formed like a tall bell tent with timber and wattled walls set on stone footings and a sloping conical thatched roof. It apparently accommodated livestock in the ring-ditch at ground level while a first floor was inserted above for family living. It consequently shows aspects of traditional building, in particular stone foundations for timber posts to prevent the feet rotting and the daubing with clay or mud of those closely aligned posts, a building tradition surviving in Easter Ross until the early part of this century. The practice of sharing the dwelling with the livestock, is similar to the longhouses of the north and west as we shall see.

spanning this great building would have been supported by its outer walls and by the huge roof trees, like cathedral columns, which divided its living space. There seems little doubt but that this was a dwelling, perhaps for a widely extended family group.

Great timber halls like Balbridie are rare (although aerial photography has shown their characteristic pattern appearing more frequently than was first thought). Archaeological information, recovered by excavation and aerial photography, shows that the most common house form for the greater part of the centuries BC was **the roundhouse.**

THE ROUNDHOUSE

Remains of these houses reveal that they were built either entirely from wood, with a circular framework of posts, or from stone footings with a timber or wattle superstructure. They would have been roofed with a combination of timber and turf or thatch. These houses, once appearing across the landscape, grouped in the hamlets or villages of the Bronze and Iron Ages, can still be seen on hillsides, their stone footings showing as heather-covered rings against a low sun. Those timber-built roundhouses leave little trace and the only evidence is sometimes their adjacent stone-lined storage compartments, previously thought to be houses themselves, the **souterrains**.

Parallel to the more simple roundhouse form there developed a range of more substantial circular buildings. Of these, the most spectacular type is the **broch,** which flourished in the last centuries BC and the first AD. The name *broch* is derived from the old Norse *borg* meaning a strong or fortified place. Brochs are peculiar to Scotland, found predominantly in the land and islands to the north and west, with a few isolated structures in the Lowlands. They are

The great broch of Mousa, Shetland (Historic Scotland).

exciting and enigmatic buildings, skilfully constructed of dry-stone masonry with massive, double-skinned walls, up to 4.5m thick, between which there are stairs, galleries and mural cells. Some, as at **Mousa** on Shetland and the **Glenelg** brochs opposite Skye, survive to more than 12m tall, with their distinctive inward batter giving them almost a modern *cooling tower* profile. Others, like those on Orkney, stand to a lesser height and may never have been as tall but still display the substantial thick walls. Most brochs have a single impressive entrance-way with often a fine

lintel slab over the doorway and a mural cell as a guardroom. The doors would have been secured by

Reconstruction of roundhouse and attached souterrain (Historic Scotland).

Wheelhouses

Other forms of substantial roundhouse include the wheelhouse, so-called from the radial piers or buttresses - like the spokes of a wheel - which re-enforce the walls, support the roof and also create between them small chambers for use as sleeping places, work spaces or for storage; the hearth lay in the centre of the room. Wheelhouses have paved floors and two of the three at Jarlshof on Shetland have additional underground stores roofed with large stone slabs and reached through short, narrow tunnels.

timber draw-bars (as we saw at Skara Brae), a feature that persists as a security measure into the 19th-century. At **Carn Liath**, Sutherland, door checks, bar-hole and guard chamber all survive.

Whether these massive constructions were intended as fortresses or simply as high status dwellings is still disputed. Internally they have the same hearths, partitioning and storage as we saw at Knap of Howar and Skara Brae at least two millennia earlier, suggesting some form of domestic role on the lines of the defensive manor house. Excavation has shown that they are not solitary towers, but the central and dominant building of a settlement comprising more modest stone huts or roundhouses. Their tower-like form can be construed as the precursor of the characteristically Scottish medieval fortified tower presaging the later domesticated manorial tower-house - early examples, then, of the *laird's house*.

JARLSHOF: CONTINUITY AND DEVELOPMENT AND THE APPEARANCE OF THE LONGHOUSE

A site which shows almost the whole range of house types we have looked at so far is **Jarlshof**, the great settlement occupying a sandstone promontory beside the shallow bay of the West Voe of Sumburgh in southern Shetland. It spans a period of 4000 years of change and development starting as far back as 2400 BC with an early building of oval shape, followed by round-houses with underground stores (one reused as a bronze-smithy) and a range of

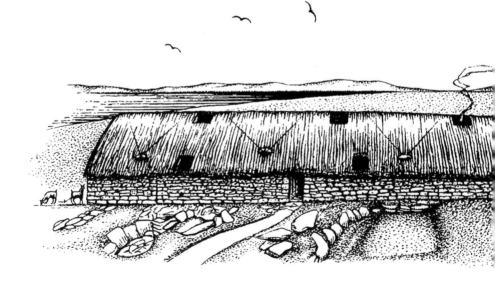

buildings including a broch and ending with the construction of a laird's tower-house in the 17th-century with its associated kiln-barn.

But long before that was built, it was the site for the other major house type: the **longhouse.** Early in the 9th century the first Norse settlers arrived, and, peaceably or otherwise impressed themselves on the Pictish residents. These Viking incomers built a large longhouse, a form that would influence dwellings in northern Scotland for many centuries to come. It was constructed mostly of turf with stone footings and probably roofed with thatch. Initially, there was a parallel barn of similar construction, but later models housed their livestock at one end, the family at the other. Similar Viking longhouses can be seen superimposed on an earlier settlement at the **Brough of Birsay** on Orkney. This is the beginning of the great tradition of the true longhouse of the north and west, humans and beast sharing a single entrance and roof.

The ensuing chapters will look at developments of the traditional houses we have seen here: the simple stone-footed types that provide the basic pattern for the humblest cottage; the longhouse that continues in many forms well into this century; the upright tower of the broch that anticipates the tower-house, and laird's house of the 16th and 17th centuries; and a whole wealth of varied forms between.

Reconstruction of a Jarlshof longhouse (Historic Scotland).

CHAPTER 3

THE VERNACULAR TRADITION

This chapter looks at the range of cottages and small farmhouses that form the basic dwellings of the Scottish countryside, continuing the traditional building forms of prehistoric antiquity, developing and adapting them through time to accommodate the lifestyles of the occupants.

OPPOSITE: Moirlanich longhouse, Perthshire. Corrugated iron has replaced the original thatch. There are two doorways, the one with a porch leads to the domestic portion of the house, the one to the left to the byre. The cottage is sited in the valley bottom, with arable land in front (now rough grass) and the hill behind, where stock would graze in summer freeing the low ground for grain, potatoes and other crops (National Trust for Scotland).

COTTAGES

The **single storey**, three-bay stone or clay-walled **cottage**, often with either contemporary or later dormered attic, is found all over Scotland, recognisable as the traditional home of the farm worker, fisherfolk, small town and village inhabitant and adapted as dwellings associated with industrial enterprises such as coal and iron mining. The survivals largely date from the 19th century, for most earlier rural and coastal predecessors have disappeared, particularly if too mean or built of more ephemeral materials such as turf or wattle.

These single-storey cottages, mainly stone-walled and slate-roofed, are all too often nowadays lost beneath unsympathetic alterations. Nevertheless, local variations are still evident. There is different stone and treatment

Regularly fronted cottage with dormers, Jemimaville, Easter Ross (Beaton).

of masonry; clay walling is common in some places. Thatched roofs, once customary, are now rare, replaced by corrugated iron, pantile or slate: there are more variations of local slates than is generally realised (as we have seen in Chapter 1). In Shetland, *tarry roofs* (tarred roofing felt) are still popular as well as in the Inner Hebrides. The position of the chimney stack, and its style, point to the relationship of the hearth with the house and can suggest date of construction. The three-bay cottage plan form is flexible, so there are larger and smaller examples with either hipped (*piended*) or gabled roofs.

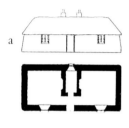

Lochaber cottages: a) two flues and mid press room; b) single flue serving two hearths (Beaton).

There is little chronological pattern for these cottages: traditional forms continued to be constructed in the Hebrides until the late 19th century. Crofters, small farmers and fisherfolk usually built their own homes, exploiting local materials and working in the traditions and techniques they knew. Enlightened landlords might provide better class housing, largely following traditional designs, though by the early 19th century the use of pattern books and architects was becoming general on country estates.

Hipped or *piended* roof cottages are common in parts of west Highland; probably a legacy of both central hearths and the gable end crucks we will look at below. In **Lochaber**, roughly between Glenelg and Ballachulish, one finds thick-walled, three-bay cottages with rounded corners, hipped roofs and central fireplaces served by large masonry flues rising in the centre of the building. There are two types, one with paired central stacks, one to each hearth serving the outer rooms, with a small (and very cosy) chamber squeezed between the two, lit by a small rear window; where there are but two rooms, these are separated by a substantial central chimney stack shared by the hearths in each room.

In Skye, the hip-roofed cottage has adapted to the gable-end hearth, most commonly by creating a flue in the gable wall, topped by a chimney stack. Alternatively the cottage has been altered by removing the roof, raising the ends as gables fitted with mural flues and apex chimney stacks, and reroofing. The tell-tale line of masonry change, rising awkwardly from the rounded corners, is often evident beneath the traditional limewash.

Where the Western Isles cottage is not linked with its associated barn and byre, it too is usually a three-bay cottage with battered walls and rounded angles. Traditional *blackhouse* walling is doubleskinned, infilled with a core of rubble or sand providing insulation and channelling excess moisture. The rafters spring from the inner edge of the wallhead, leaving a wide verge which in time becomes green with grass providing grazing for agile sheep.

Hinging lums

The hanging chimney was a wooden or mud-daubed wicker canopy dooked (pegged) against the gable wall, usually supported by projecting wooden cheeks. This canopy was continuous with the tapering timber flue abutting the gable, rising through the ridge as a chimney — not a conventional masonry stack but either a square wooden box or a wooden frame covered with thatch and daubed with clay as fire precaution. As peat does not give out sparks, flue and chimney were safer than might at first appear. The presence of a hinging lum can easily be recognised from outside the house by the position of the chimney stack perched on the ridge inwards from the gable apex as seen in the example from Strathspey on the left. These have usually been replaced in brick, stone or even, as in this case, by tin.

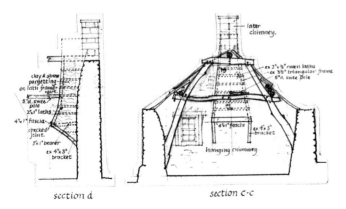

Cross section and elevation showing the construction of a 'hinging lum' (Royal Commission on the Ancient and Historical Monuments of Scotland).

section d   section c-c

In **Tiree**, where the island is flat and the winds are strong, the cottage walls are immensely thick – around 1.65m-1.92m (5ft 6in) and also doubleskinned, with sand as an infilling between the outer wall, *am balla-mach* and the inner wall, *am balla-staig:* there is also a wide ledge, *an tobhta.* The windows are well sheltered, almost hidden in the depth of the wall, the small panes of glass glinting between tunnel-like cheeks. Cottages were thatched on fertile Tiree, but tarred felt roofs are also part of the island building tradition.

CRUCK-FRAMED COTTAGES

Cruck framing, whereby a pairs of wooden cruck trusses (*highland couples* in the north, *siles* in Ayrshire, Renfrewshire and Roxburghshire) supported the roof was a construction feature through most of Scotland except in Orkney, Shetland and the Western Isles where timber was scarce. The lower ends of the cruck blades rest on a stone plinth providing a sound foundation and preventing rot through damp. The sophistication of cruck-truss carpentry varies from area to area according to the timber available: where there was ample wood, elegant single piece crucks could be constructed; elsewhere the trusses were jointed, usually two sections of timber tenoned and pegged at the *elbow* where the truss curves into the roofline from the wallhead. The characteristic rounded ridge

Cruck-framed cottage, Torthorwald (Historic Scotland).

line of Caithness thatched cottages comes from the hooped form of the supporting composite cruck-frames, often many small pieces linked together. Gable end or *hip* crucks are incorporated in some buildings, giving added support to heavy thatch, notably in the Ardnamurchan peninsula, Argyll. Here, as elsewhere, the hipped or *piended* roof is a legacy of the central hearth, though later adaptations accommodate the mural flue.

Cruck-framed cottages are usually single-storey, three-bay dwellings often visually no different externally from dwellings with masonry walls sufficiently strong to carry the entire weight of the roof. They tended to be low, particularly where timber was in short supply and the cruck frames of composite construction. Though mainly a rural characteristic, cruck-framing is found in towns. In 1988, a single cruck blade, all that remained from a cruck framed cottage in a narrow passage close, was identified in the centre of Elgin in Moray.

Torthorwald cruck-framed cottage, Dumfriess-shire. Isometric drawing revealing the cruck-framed structure, the feet of the cruck blades set in the base of the rubble stone walls, thus preventing rotting on damp soil. The upper portion of this wooden framework is covered with turf sods as an underlay for thatch. The 'hinging lum' abuts the gable wall, top left (Royal Commission on the Ancient and Historical Monuments of Scotland).

THE LONGHOUSE

The **longhouse**, as its name implies, is an elongated dwelling with accommodation for people and their livestock under one roof. They have a long European tradition exported from Scandinavia to Ireland (Irish *byre-dwellings*), Greenland and the Northern Isles of Britain. Longhouses have been identified in England, where there is a wide medieval distribution, and were common in Wales.

In Scotland, longhouses were common in the north and west and in the Northern and Western Isles and were still in use well into this century. Like those we saw at Jarlshof, the buildings were single storey, varying in length and accommodation (for both family and agricultural purposes) from area to area. In Orkney and Caithness they are literally '*long* houses' combining not only simple domestic space, but also byres, stable, barn and corn-drying kiln. In Argyll they

Longhouse, 42 Arnol, Lewis, Western Isles. A thick-walled Western Isles longhouse with single byre and house entry used by both beasts and residents; a parallel barn lies at the rear (see plan below) (Historic Scotland).

Plan, 42 Arnol. The only window lights the sleeping room; other rooms are lit by rooflights. The blocked winnowing hole, 'toll fhasgnaida', to ensure draught to blow away chaff when winnowing corn is immediately left of (rear) barn door. There is a mural byre-drain in the byre gable. The layout gave storage room for family as well as fodder for beasts; the latter could be tended without going out of doors, a blessing in stormy winter weather (Historic Scotland).

tend to be shorter, with just a **domestic area** and **byre** while there is a specialised form in the Western Isles, where they are also shorter, the barn often added at the back but with access from the front range.

These various longhouse forms evolved from the nature of farming with which the houses were associated. In Orkney and Caithness they were on improved and usually owner-occupied land; others were often part of a township group of individual crofting tenants. Auchindrain, Argyll, is notable as a joint-tenancy township.

The rural parish minister gained much of his living through farming the glebe and his manse was similar to contemporary better quality farmhouses. Donald Sage described the longhouse into which his grandfather, The Revd Aeneas Sage, Minister of Lochcarron, Wester Ross, moved in 1726:

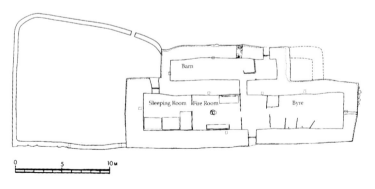

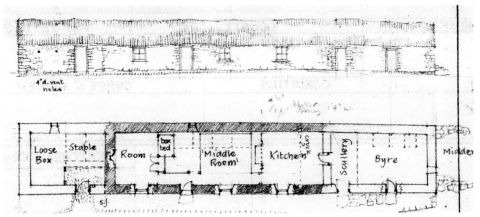

The manse of Lochcarron to which my grandfather conducted his young wife was a humble fabric...The manse was constructed after the fashion of all Highland houses about the end of the seventeenth century. About 100 feet long, the walls were built of stone for about three feet in height above the foundation and around the roots of the couples, which were previously fixed to the ground; over this were several layers of turf or fail, so as to bring the wall to the height of 10 feet. The whole was then thatched with heather. This long building was divided into several apartments; the first was called the chamber, where there was a chimney at one end, a small glazed window looking to the south, and a tent bed inserted into the partition which divided it from the next room. In this apartment the heads of the family sat and took their meals. The bed in it was usually appropriated for guests; the next apartment contained tent beds for the junior branches, with an entry door by which access to the principal apartment was provided for the heads of the family as well as for their guests. This second apartment opened into a third, where the heads of the family slept. Next came what was called the 'cearn' (or servants' hall). This compartment of the Highland house, or 'tigh slathait', was larger or longer than the others. It had cross lights, namely, a small boarded window on each side. The fireplace was usually an old mill-stone placed in the centre of the apartment, on which the peat-fire was fenced with a basket of wicker work open at both ends. Around the fire sat the servants, and in the farmers' houses, the heads of the family, along with their children. Divided from the 'cearn' and often by a very slender partition, and as the last division of the tenement, was the cow-house (or byre) occupying at least 50 feet of the entire length.

Laidhay, Caithness. Late 18th-early 19th-century cruck-framed longhouse with later stable and probably rebuilt byre, all in linear formation. An original single entrance now leads to the scullery (later adapted from a portion of the byre). Originally the kitchen communicated directly with the byre. Note the gable mural byre-drain to the midden. Ridge chimneys serving 'Room' and kitchen re-constructed c.1980 when Laidhay became a museum (Royal Commission on the Ancient and Historical Monuments of Scotland).

This description is quoted in full because it gives so much information about the allocation of space between family and livestock, and how that space was used. If Donald Sage was correct with his measurements, family and servants occupied four rooms taking up one half of the longhouse, a generous building about 100ft long and 20ft wide (approximately 31m × 6m). The width is dictated

Byre at 42 Arnol, Lewis, linked to the kitchen by a door (Historic Scotland).

by the cruck truss span: in the West Coast parishes of Lochcarron (also Lochalsh, Kintail, Glenshiel and Glenelg) there was a tradition of large cruck-framed buildings, still surviving as barns peculiar to the area. The **kitchen** in the Lochcarron Manse was in the centre of the building, the heart of the house, divided by a 'slender partition' from the byre at one side and the three family rooms on the other. This was the only room with two windows, one in each outer wall and both unglazed. However, there was a glazed window in the best chamber. Sage does not specify whether there was a single entry for man and beast, though this would have been likely, the common doorway enabling cattle to turn into the byre one way and the human occupants the other. The practice of single entry died away from the 18th century onwards, depending on location, to be replaced by separate doorways but with internal communication between kitchen and byre.

Though these longhouses have disappeared from Wester Ross, the type survives locally as long, high cruck-framed **barns** with wide wickerwork or louvred mural panels for ventilation, necessary in the damp climate of this area of high rainfall. In these barns, successors to the longhouse, we have a continuation of both the cruck-framed tradition and the use of wattle.

These linear houses are still evident in Caithness and Orkney: they were common in Sutherland and throughout upland rural areas where cattle (rather than arable) formed the backbone of the farming economy, where harsher climatic conditions demanded that the valuable beasts be over-wintered indoors. Albeit seemingly primitive, the single building was less demanding on heat and ensured the care of their vital stock by the farming family. They continued to be constructed until the end of the 19th century in the north and west. Though the Crofters Holdings (Scotland) Act of 1886 gave the crofter security of his land, he was expected to provide his own house... which he did, usually of traditional form. In Lewis new blackhouses were being built at least until 1898, combining domestic and byre accommodation. **Maidenloch**, 120, Clachtoll on the west coast of Sutherland, was only abandoned as a home around 1954.

An unusual cluster of longhouses was at Broubster Square, near Reay, Caithness, built in 1839 as a hollow square, of which only three sides survive. The complex was established to house families relocated from the Broubster and Shurrery estates; one cottage was lived in until 1960. Mural slots, in which the cruck trusses would have rested, suggest that at least one of the surviving dwellings was cruck framed. These slots were infilled, indicating renewal of the roof structure at a later date. At Broubster we have traditional buildings sited in a formal manner as a diminutive planned village, the layout apparently dictated by the landowner (see Chapter 7).

INTERNAL FEATURES: HEARTHS, BEDS, WINDOWS AND DOORS

The central **hearth** survived longest in Shetland, Orkney and the Western Isles. As at the 18th-century Lochcarron Manse described above, the usual base was a millstone, while the wicker basket at Lochcarron might have been a circular hanging canopy intended to draw the smoke upwards. Peat was the usual fuel: it will burn at ground level, unlike coal which requires a draught under the fire. Sage described how farming families would sit together around the fire, a reminder that this played many roles: it provided heat for cooking, light and warmth, it consumed rubbish while the ashes were a valuable nutrient for the land. The hearth was the heart of the house, where the occupants would sit, eat, work, talk: the heads of the family had their own chairs, the others sat on stools or the *restin' chair,* a long bench with back and arms which doubled as a bed. This *muckle chair* is a *being* or *seiseach* in Gaelic, a *deece* in north-east Scotland and

Interior of the domestic quarters at 42 Arnol, Lewis, with a kettle suspended over the central hearth, dressers to the side and a view through the open door leading to the byre (Historic Scotland).

the *langsettle* in Lanarkshire, a lowland Scots form of the English farmhouse *settle*.

Central hearths sometimes had a *back*, a flagstone or low wall constructed between the fire and the doorway to help control draught and as a useful place to stand kettle or other utensils. The back stone survived well into this century in Orkney and Shetland.

The gable fireplace coexisted with the central hearth if there was a best *chamber*, where it served for warmth rather than cooking, superseding the fire in the middle of the room from the 18th century onwards. For this there is no fixed time-scale: circumstances, traditions, and changes varied from place to place. The gable hearth required a flue and chimney: hollowing out a mural flue was at times impracticable: sparsely mortared masonry or clay walling could be unsuitable for such a cavity. Here the common form was the *hinging lum* which we have seen.

Other than in the bakehouses of castles and mansions, built ovens of stone or clay were not found in the lesser Scottish house. Here Scotland is similar to Ireland but different from elsewhere in the British Isles and northern Europe. Traditional Scottish oatcakes and bannocks were baked on a flat iron girdle (and probably once a heated stone). Similarly stews, broth and soup could simmer beside or over the fire.

The girdle or cooking pot was hung above the central hearth on a *crook* suspended either from the rafters or a cross beam inserted for the purpose. For the gable hearth a similar, usually iron, beam was placed across the flue over the fire but this was awkward for movement of cooking utensils. The *swey*, already common in the greater house, came into general use. These are right-angled, pivoting metal arms installed to one side of the hearth, manufactured both by local blacksmiths and commercial iron foundries.

Box beds

We can look to prehistory for the earliest **box bed**. In the earliest of the series of dwellings at Skara Brae there are mural alcoves which served as beds: in the later huts the beds were stone structures on each side of the central hearth. They were filled with heather or other dried vegetable matter and skins for warmth.

More recently, box beds were not limited to cottages occupied by lesser folk; fine examples with panelled fronts survive from the 18th century at Udrigle, Gairloch, Wester Ross and Ballantruan, Avonside, Banffshire. They were an integral part of the Scottish house, exploiting limited room space and often serving as room dividers, sometimes instead of fixed party walling. They were usually in rooms that were heated, particularly the kitchen. The beds were closed with hinged or sliding doors, or by curtains drawn to give privacy.

Curtained box bed in the kitchen of Barries' birthplace, Kirriemuir, Angus (Beaton).

Windows and doors

Wooden **shutters** or **hurdles** were common in rural cottages until the turn of the 1800s. Where there were windows, these were very small: some rooms were lit by the open door or by the smoke-hole later replaced by a chimney. Stretched **sheepskins**, with their wool removed and mounted on a frame, were a substitute for glass.

Auchmithie, Angus.
Fisherfolk bating
lines - men, women and
children all involved.
The cottages are roofed
with heavy Angus slates
(Angus Council).

Many late 19th-century photographers captured records of women spinning at their doorstep or fisherfolk busy with baiting the lines, outside their cottage homes. While the latter obviously kept the mess and smell of bait away from the house and was part of the close-knit working/social life of the fisher families, the location of the spinning wheel more obviously points to poor light in the home due to **small windows** (although by the time the photographer was busy, multi-pane, vertical sliding sash windows had been inserted in most cottages).

Doors were, in the past, also closed with hurdles. These were similar to the interwoven ventilation panels in the large barns of Wester Ross and Inverness-shire. A traditional type was the double-leaf plank door: an adequate entry was feasible by opening one leaf only, keeping the warmth in and inclement weather out. Both leaves could be opened in fine weather for more generous passage of people, furniture or goods. Sadly many of these sturdy doors have been awkwardly replaced by standard DIY models.

Attic lights and dormer windows

Exploitation of **attic** space, whether for storage or sleeping accommodation (or both) was obviously necessary in small cottages. Tiny gable windows lit these spaces, often blocked where later dormer windows have been inserted. Small swept dormers could be accommodated by thatch but were more awkward when the roof was pantiled or slated. Another source of attic light was the skylight; these were manufactured by iron-foundries and became widespread from mid-19th century with improved rail transport. In areas of flagstone, particularly Orkney and Caithness, square holes are cut into flagstone, glazed and fitted in roofs as fixed lights.

The variety of Scottish **dormers** is infinite. For cottages, small hipped, swepped or piended dormers can be original or later insertions – there is no mistaking that over-large 'box dormers' are recent. As demands for more accommodation increased, houses were often built at one-and-a-half storey height, the upper floor lit by windows breaking the wallhead, rising as gabled dormers. Gable apices could be decorated either with carved stone or a decorative cast-iron finials. This gabled-dormer tradition was part of the 16th- and 17th-century tower-house and merchant house vocabulary which we will see below, gradually working itself down the social scale to become a familiar sight in town and country from the mid-19th century onwards.

Late 19th-century one-and-a-half-storey house in Rothiemay, Banffshire (Beaton). The attic storey was lit by the canted wallhead and small centre piended dormers. Note the pale local Avochie granite frontage with contrasting dark pinnings (Aberdeen Bonding) and the ornate cast-iron railings and decorative dormer finials increasingly available through the expanding rail network. The double windows (bipartites) were glazed with large panes of glass (see pp. 20, 72), also transported by rail.

We have looked at the variations of the simple cottage, together with the longhouse and some permanent furnishings, part of a long tradition stretching back to the prehistoric houses which can still be seen in the isles of Orkney and Shetland. In the next chapter another tradition unfolds – the tower-house as the domesticated successor to the defensive castle.

CHAPTER 4

TOWER-HOUSES

LAIRDS' HOMES OF THE

16TH AND 17TH CENTURIES

In this chapter we look at the traditional tower-house, a domesticated version of the native fortified castle with a vertical emphasis echoing the broch towers of later prehistory.

Medieval castles as fortified buildings rather than homes are outwith the scope of this book. Long after their defensive role was obsolete, the castellated, stylistic influence persisted, but with scant or no provision for fire-power. The post-Reformation **tower-house**, a domesticated version of the native fortified castle, blossomed in the mid-16th century, the medieval vertical form transformed and adapted to provide more comfortable and spacious accommodation. Confusingly, they are often called *castles* – for example **Crathes** Castle, **Scalloway** Castle – but this must not detract from the overall domestic nature and manorial status of the tower-house, despite vestigial defensive elements. Sometimes *tower* survives in their title, as at **Amisfield** Tower or **Coxton** Tower; even more confusingly, the latter was referred to in early 17th-century as *fortalice and manor place*. The term *palace* was occasionally used in contemporary 16th- and 17th-century literature when referring to specific buildings of this type, and was introduced to The Palace, **Culross** in the 19th century, a misleading term for an albeit prosperous town-house.

After the Reformation of 1560, secular wealth which had previously been spent either on fortification or the provision and upkeep of chapels and monasteries, was freed for other purposes. Church lands became available for redistribution, much of it exploited and divided as small estates by *bonnet lairds* (small land-owners) and by the rising class of moneyed merchants whose entrepreneurial skills and overseas trading ventures generated the

OPPOSITE: *Muckrach Castle, Inverness-shire (Beaton). L-plan tower-house built by Patrick Grant of Freuchie (Castle Grant, Grantown-on-Spey). The doorway is sited traditionally in the angle of the L: above it is a stone plaque dated 1598, the arms of Patrick Grant and his wife Margaret Stewart and the motto 'IN GOD IS ALL MY TRAIST'. The principal room on the first floor is indicated by a larger window and is reached by a wheel-stair in the tower to the left of the entrance. The upper rooms are accessed by the narrow stair tower projecting from the angle; note the angle bartizan at the right commanding the rear approaches. The tower-house stands on a spur overlooking the valley and surrounding country.*

Smailholm Tower,
Roxburghshire, a simple
tower of the 15th or
possibly 16th century
(Historic Scotland).

means to indulge in more spacious and fashionable homes. The introduction of *feu-farming,* with heritable tenures, gave tenants and cadet members of greater families security of occupation and fostered the assumption that house and land would pass to their successors. This encouraged long-term improvements and the construction of durable dwelling houses of stone and lime, in contrast to the impermanent homes and humbler huts of the poor.

STYLE AND LAYOUT

It was understandable that these bonnet lairds would aspire, albeit on a smaller scale, to the precedence of architectural style established by their forebears, the heads of families and larger landowners, with seats in the older, often massive medieval towers. The new home was constructed in time-honoured vertical tradition, emulating the earlier defensive tower but with room for family privacy and greater domestic comfort. Where more horizontal floor space was required than was possible within the confines of the single tower, this was provided by the simple expedient of abutting another vertical unit, creating either an **L-plan**, or if two towers were added diagonally, a **Z-plan** form. Within this simple alphabetical terminology there are

First-floor plans of rectangular, L-plan and Z-plan towers (Historic Scotland)

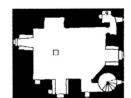

Smailholm, Roxburghshire

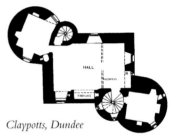

Scalloway Castle, Shetland

Claypotts, Dundee

Claypots Z-plan Castle, Dundee (Historic Scotland).

many variations, each building individual but with the recognisable architectural vocabulary and form of the post-Reformation tower-house. The medieval way of life was long-lived in Scotland, for medieval craftsmanship persisted until well into the 1600s, enhanced and developed by the infiltration of continental influence of which many of the mercantile and landowning builders became increasingly aware.

Fordyce Castle, Banffshire 1592, in centre of Fordyce village (Beaton).

These 16th- and early 17th-century tower-houses are built of rubble masonry, sometimes harled, with dressed stone door and window margins besides the decorative detailing of carved dormer pediments, corbelling and chimney-heads. They rise three, four or five storeys high, austerely plain and windowless at ground floor level but with the **first-floor hall** (principal room) expressed externally by a larger window. If L- or Z-plan, the sole doorway is

Cut-open reconstructon of Smailholm Tower. This 15th/16th-century tower has been adapted over the centuries and other accommodation added within the confines of the courtyard or barmkin. The vaulted ground floor, where the entrance is guarded by an iron yett, is used for storage; goods were hauled to the first-floor hall through a hatch. Though cooking is illustrated in the first-floor hall, there was also an outside kitchen. The Laird's private room with bed was on the second floor and there was an attic chamber in the roof. All rooms were reached by a stone wheel – or turnpike stair (Historic Scotland).

normally within the angle formed by the extruding wing against the main tower, the most secure position for this vulnerable opening, usually covered by a shot-hole or two, either to intimidate would-be aggressors or as a status symbol – or even both. Other shot-holes, sometimes decorative in shape and detailing, may puncture the sides of the bartizans or the walling below windows. Additional security and privacy were ensured by the enclosing wall (*barmkin*), perhaps entered through an arched gateway. It is at the upper level that the character of the Renaissance building is expressed; exotic angle turrets (*bartizans*) project on carved corbelling to rise above wallhead height; there are ornate, pedimented dormer-heads with dates and monograms, convex stair turrets extrude from the wallface; skilfully inserted oriel windows command wide panoramas for the residents; gables are crowstepped and pierced with small attic lights and the chimney stacks are tall and coped. These features, either individually or orchestrated over the full repertoire, reveal either the austerity or the complexity of the individual building. In Aberdeenshire and Kincardineshire, in particular, these upper works, designed to be viewed from all angles, flower in profusion in a group of early 17th-century castellated towers - Crathes, Castle Fraser and others - the high point of the Scottish manorial tower-house.

Corbelled base to stair turret, Fordyce Castle, 1592 (Beaton).

This early 17th-century flowering fostered manorial castles whose conventional layout provided comfortable rooms and easy internal movement. Domesticated **Muchalls** Castle, Kincardineshire (1619–1627), built around two sides of a walled courtyard but only two storeys high, has a vaulted ground floor providing service accommodation while the upper floor allowed a generous living space, some rooms handsomely decorated with fine plaster ceilings. Any defence is concentrated on the arched entrance to the courtyard, which is guarded by gun-loops and curious vestigial open bartizans. The courtyard, successor to the barmkin, lingered on throughout the 17th century, particularly in the merchant houses of Orkney.

Despite the increased accommodation and comfort devised within the various layouts, there was still room for the simple square tower and for this, as for all these buildings, there is little neat chronological stylistic order within the hundred years from 1560-1660: new forms

Plan and view of Muchalls Castle, Kincardineshire, an L-plan laird's house enclosed by walled courtyard or barmkin 1619–1627 (MacGibbon and Ross, Castellated and Domestic Architecture of Scotland, ii).

and anachronisms abounded side by side. **Amisfield**, Dumfries-shire (1600) is virtually square and four storeys high; yet the crowded roofscape is highly developed with corbelling, bartizans, caphouse and tall chimney stacks. At the opposite end of the country, **Coxton** Tower, near Elgin, is a simple early 17th-century laird's tower apparently founded by Sir Alexander Innes, the tower completed c.1640 by his grandson, also Sir Alexander. Four plain vaulted rooms are piled one on top of the other terminating with a double-pitched sandstone slab-covered roof. A simple corbelled bartizan projects at two opposed angles with an open balcony at the third angle; these are the only extrusions alleviating the austere lines of the tower. The main entrance is at first-floor level, originally reached by withdrawable ladder (the masonry forestair was added in the 19th century) while the narrow stairs linking each floor are burrowed in the depth of the mural masonry, each room originally communicating with the vaulted cellar via a hatch in the floor/ceiling through which supplies could be raised or lowered. Thus this Morayshire laird constructed for himself a four-roomed, fireproof masonry tower, a near contemporary with the Renaissance sophistication of manorial tower-houses, and with the neighbouring innovative Innes House, yet just as suited to the needs and fashion of two centuries earlier.

Early 17th-century turnpike or wheel staircase (Beaton).

DOORWAYS, STAIRS AND WINDOWS

Above or near the main doorway of a post-Reformation tower-house there might be a **datestone** recording the names or initials of the owner/builders and date of the house, a text or armorial. Security would be re-enforced by a *yett*, a peculiarly Scottish hinged and inward-opening interlacing iron grille mounted immediately behind the main door. The entrance leads into a vaulted ground floor (the vaulting strengthens the building) and to a staircase leading to the first (principal) floor; a wide **wheel-stair** fills a circular tower as at **Kilcoy**, Ross-shire or a dog-leg if the staircase is housed in a square well. Wide staircases of whatever type are often limited between ground and first floor; thereafter, the space above is devoted to small rooms while access to upper floors continues by narrow stairs within the wall thickness or smaller wheel-stairs housed in partially projecting mural towers.

The principal room in a laird's tower-house, the first-floor hall, is lit by larger windows than other rooms. The ceiling could be plainly vaulted as at Coxton with few fittings other than a hearth, mural cupboard or *aumbry* and an alcove for a candle or lamp. More complex structures might be more elaborately decorated with either painted timber or moulded plaster ceiling, large fireplace with plain or carved stone chimney-piece and panelled walls. The number of other rooms depends entirely on the size of the building. Perhaps simply two or three rooms above the first floor hall with additional space squeezed into the attic or a range of rooms, each floor linked by mural wheel-stairs. In the Z-plan type, these intercommunicating staircases are usually paired, neatly slotted into circular mural voids between the central square and flanking towers.

Painted and plaster ceilings

The period 1560-1660 coincides with the vigorous Scottish **painted ceiling**, superseded in the first half of the 17th century by plasterwork. For painting, a water soluble tempera paint with added glue for binding power and coloured with vegetable pigments produced a vivid, translucent yet matt surface; the painted decoration was applied to the beams, intermediate joists and tongue-and-grooved boards, or sometimes to a wooden vault nailed to invisible supporting timbers. The colours were bright and the range of design

A 16th-century painted ceiling at Huntingtower Castle, Perthshire. The intersecting design is repeated on the beams and joists (Historic Scotland).

wide, based on a variety of European pattern influences. **Prestongrange** (1581, now removed to Merchiston Tower, Edinburgh) is Italianate and executed in subtle shades of pink, terracotta and white, while bolder work at **Crathes** Castle, Kincardineshire felicitously portrays musicians, kings and noblemen in linear design between lattice and scroll-painted joists.

Plaster ceilings began to gain popularity in the early 17th century, the English fashion of exuberant and sophisticated three-dimensional white relief ornament superseding the exotic colouring of the tempera painting as ceiling and wall decoration. Some decorative themes survived and remained constant: the Nine Worthies, with David and Alexander as favourites, were modelled as roundels within strapwork cartouches and geometric ribs, their images reappearing as itinerant plasterers travelled with their moulds and their handiwork from one location to another. The plaster was formed from a mixture of sand, lime, water and chopped animal hair.

Deep friezes and magnificent overmantels with armorials were also the product of the plasterer's art. Motifs such as thistles, Tudor roses and fleurs-de-lys indicated support for the Union while family crests and monograms were incorporated. These white ceilings made the rooms lighter, enhancing large principal apartments and small chambers alike.

VARIATIONS ON THE THEME: PELE TOWERS AND BASTLES

Though the defensive characteristics of these tower-houses of manifold shape, size and plan-form were of stylistic character rather

than 'for real', in the border country between Scotland and England, where cattle *reiving* (raiding) was commonplace, **pele towers** and **bastles** were constructed as fortalices in times of local troubles and as protective buildings where cattle could be gathered for safe keeping in times of insecurity. The practice of taking refuge when threatened by sudden raid was common both sides of the border; the places of refuge tended to be in groups with walled enclosures within which livestock could be confined. In Dumfriesshire, some

Darnick Tower, Melrose, Roxburghshire, a surviving Border pele tower (Historic Scotland).

tower-houses were provided with **beacon platforms** at the wallhead, the fire beacons forming part of a signalling system in times of border conflict to '…never faill burning so long as the Englishmen remain in Scotland'.

At **Ardclach** in inland Nairnshire, there is a two-storey *belltower*, a diminutive tower-house furnished with shot holes, dated 1655 and perched on a knoll overlooking the River Findhorn and the former parish church with the moors of Braemoray and the Cairngorms beyond. Cattle rearing was a major local occupation: the marauding forays of the Alexander Stewart, *Wolf of Badenoch,* in the late 14th century and his successors from Lochindorb Castle not far south and the later activities of cattle thieves suggest that the tower might be a northern *pele tower* combining the defensive and watchtower roles with that of belltower.

Bastles

The *bastel-house* or **bastle** (French *bastille*) was a defensive farmhouse found on both sides of the border. They consisted of a basement, usually barrel-vaulted, with a single storey above. Usually there were two entrances, one in the ground floor for animals and provisions, the other reached by either an internal or external stair; doorways were fitted with strong draw-bars and windows with iron bars. The village of Lesmudden in Roxburghshire is said to have had 16 of these in the mid-16th century. An interesting scatter of bastles has recently been located in the Upper Clyde and Tweed valleys, dating from the early 1600s, establishing bastles 40 miles north of the Scottish border. Like their English counterparts, these are all oblong in plan, with barrel-vaulted ground floor and chamber above reached by internal or external stair. The walls are thick, some times less so for the upper storey, and the roofs slated: doorways are re-enforced with draw-bars and windows have traces of iron grills. The design of these houses is for security and defence, reflecting a new found wealth to be protected and suggesting the emergence in the early 17th century of reasonably prosperous tenant farmers, anticipating bonnet lairds.

Old Skelbo House, Dornoch, Sutherland. An unusual and important Highland bastle, constructed c.1600 as successor to medieval Skelbo Castle, sited within the castle enclosure. Livestock were accommodated in the vaulted ground floor which has byre drainage: domestic quarters were in the first floor and attic, reached by a forestair (Royal Commission on the Ancient and Historical Monuments of Scotland).

Having looked at the tower-houses it is important to stress the varied nature of this entirely individual range of Scottish vernacular castellated manors. Many occupy earlier fortified sites, some have elements of fortification, others are large and imposing and contrast with those that are entirely domestic in scale.

CHAPTER 5

LAIRDS' AND MERCHANTS' HOUSES

17TH–18TH CENTURIES

I n this chapter we look at the houses of the well to-do, the burgh merchant, the small landowner, the ship's captain, the lawyer. The spread is wider, the buildings usually smaller than many of the tower-houses cited in the previous chapter and a fashionable symmetry begins to influence house design.

THE DEMISE OF THE TOWER-HOUSE

By the second half of the 17th century, the tower-house was passing out of favour for, according to Lord Strathmore, 'such houses truly are worn quyt out of fashione, as feuds are, which is a great happiness'. Leslie Castle, Aberdeenshire (1661) is amongst the last – here the defensive vocabulary of bartizans and gun-loops displayed may have been as much for show as for insurance against local strife: the great stair tower extruding from one angle is both a status symbol and a domestic convenience.

In 1623, about the same time as Alexander of Burnett Leys and his son, Sir Thomas, were building Muchalls Castle, William Monteith of Randieford erected his homely Hill House in Dunfermline, with its canted stair tower tucked into the angle of the L-plan. A generation later, between 1640 and 1653, Sir Robert Innes of Innes, built his splendid mansion of **Innes House** along traditional lines but with the elevations defined with regular windows and bandcourses. Apparently convinced that his Moray homeland was peaceful, the

OPPOSITE: *Langskaill, completed by 1676, on the shores of the small island of Gairsay, Orkney, had a U-plan range closed by a screen wall (originally balustraded) linked to the gable ends of the domestic buildings; this wall is pierced by a fine round-headed archway, enriched with a carved relief of trailing vine and grapes, flanked by shot-holes and topped by a pedimented armorial. Langskaill is a marvellous combination of the defensive and the domestic aspects of a laird's house in the Orkney tradition (Rendall).*

Innes House, by Elgin.
(1640-53). Sir Robert
commissioned William Ayton,
master mason, Edinburgh, to
'draw the forme of the house in
paper' for which he was paid
£26.13d (Scots). Ayton kept to
the traditional L-plan, but
installed symmetrical fenestration,
the large windows linked with
horizontal ashlar string courses
(narrow ashlar fillets) to stress the
emergent classical emphasis.
It was buit of local harled rubble
with liberal use of fine sandstone
ashlar dressings and
ornamentation. The sandstone
came from highly regarded coastal
Covesea quarries, six miles or so
westward, from whence it was
brought by boat to Speyslaw,
the nearest point to Innes, the
transport costing between three
and four times the price of the
stone. Iron came from Leith,
wood from Glen Moriston,
Inverness-shire and 'twantie,
two thousand, skleatts' from
Caithness. The slater was paid for
'thatcking (thatching) my house',
the verb synonymous with
slating.

sole defence was a couple of gun-loops in time-honoured position close to the entrance. The house, one of the most remarkable *lairds' houses* of its time, comprised a main four-storey block and wing with a projecting, pinnacled and balustraded stair tower rising above the ridge, housing a stone dog-leg staircase. In it, as in so many more, the vertical emphasis of the tower-house tradition is still evident and lingers on into the second half of the 17th century. In other respects the buildings are forward-looking, stylistically coming to terms with, and being influenced by, the new and **fashionable symmetry** of both elevation and layout, with its regular disposition of windows and doors.

While Innes may be a forerunner of the country-house, if in a vernacular mould, the same layout was practical for more modest dwellings, providing two or more rooms to each floor with staircase communication. Ford House, Midlothian, 1680, is just two storeys and attic with canted angle stairtower: '...a most attractive example of its kind, the douce harled walls and wayward roof-line giving it an informal quality wholly appropriate to its purpose and situation' (J G Dunbar, 1966).

Scattered throughout Scotland there are others of this type, in different shapes and sizes, large and small: delightful, sometimes quirky, always pleasing. Many will have been enlarged and altered but original features of the 16th and 17th centuries are often still recognisable.

BURGH MERCHANTS' HOUSES

Seventeenth-century burgh merchants exploited congested plots of land in prime street locations to provide commercial and storage premises in the ground floor with domestic accommodation above, the latter lit with regular windows, the former arcaded or furnished with small shuttered lights. A circular stair tower could abut the frontage, imposing on the street as at 16/18 Shore Street, **Thurso**, Caithness (dated 1686), or at the rear where there was space to accommodate this extrusion as at 1 High Shore, **Banff**.

Dated 1675 this three-storey house is a combination of the turreted tower-house tradition and classical symmetry. The house occupies a corner site in High Shore, originally the heart of Banff. The ground floor is quite plain with the door in the centre; three regularly disposed windows light the first floor, swept dormers break the wallhead above. The street angle is adorned with a projecting bartizan, undoubtedly a status symbol, but extremely practical as a viewing place from which to command the comings and goings in the street and church opposite. A substantial, circular stair tower abuts the back of the house, terminating in a corbelled square, gabled and crowstepped caphouse within the rear court. Ingleneuk, Waterpath is another merchant house in Banff, of varying 17th/18th-century date, entered from the street through a deep round-headed archway with domestic accommodation above. The deep ingleneuk hearth, still the focus of the kitchen in the earliest part of the house, is served by a massive chimney stack. It is close to the commercial heart of the burgh so business could be carried on in privacy and goods stored and handled away from the street. Similar houses can be found in many Scottish burghs whose prosperity was built on trade.

ARCADED FRONTAGES

Where there was no room or provision for an inner court, the **arcaded frontage**, supporting additional first-floor accommodation, offered shelter and sometimes access to a wynd or passage to the rear. In **Elgin**, Moray, three such late 17th-century houses survive in the High Street from a rich group now known only through contemporary illustrations. One is dated 1688 and two 1694; all have arcaded ground-floor frontages and regular fenestration in the upper two storeys. The street arcades are supported by squat pillars with square capitals enriched by simple, almost naive detailing: the window margins are moulded and the gables crowstepped: there are gabletted or swept dormers, and some original local sandstone slab roofing. The gable-end chimney stacks have the deep, corniced copes of their time. There are

Braco's Banking House, Elgin, Moray, 1694. Pend at right leads to rear court (Beaton).

similar houses in High Street, **Lithlithgow** with round-arched access to the rear.

Provost Ross's House, Shiprow, Aberdeen is a tall, late 16th-century L-plan house with an arcaded extension of a century later. Sited close by the harbour, it is entered straight from the street into shallow, screen-walled court The little room at the top of the projecting tower wing has windows on all sides commanding harbour and town. This and other merchant houses were built well into the 18th century as trade prospered at home and abroad. As street frontage became scarcer and more costly, the arcade became the pend arch, giving access to the rear of the property.

CULROSS AND THE EAST NEUK OF FIFE

The Palace, Culross and the Firth of Forth (National Trust for Scotland)

To experience the merchant houses of the period, a visit to **Culross**, Fife is well worthwhile. The narrow cobbled streets are lined with small houses, most still homes but some open to the

public. Mercantile activity, trade and coalmining, centred on the Forth estuary fostered at Culross by the entrepreneur Sir George Bruce, encouraged development and created sufficient prosperity to

Pedimented dormers, 1611, north block, The Palace, Culross (National Trust for Scotland).

build good homes by the standards of the time. The restoration of original fabric over the past decades has ensured the survival of this charming small burgh with houses from late 16th to the 18th century occupying the

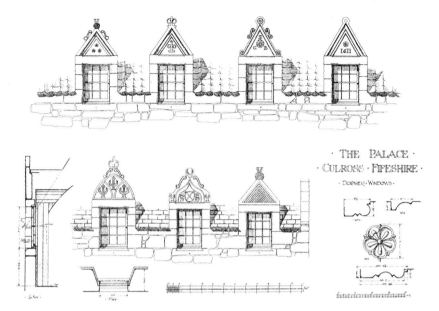

· THE · PALACE ·
· CULROSS · FIFESHIRE ·
· DORMER · WINDOWS ·

level terrain by the shore and sprawling up the steep hillside. Crowsteps, pantile roofs, painted ceilings, carved dormers, corbelled towers and rear walled-gardens are all there. Within walking distance one can see more of 17th-century Scottish small burgh architecture than anywhere else.

St Monance, Pittenweem, Astruther and Crail crowd the southern shore of the **East Neuk of Fife**. Originally these towns developed and became prosperous through trade, largely with the Low Countries, though the harbours, particularly Pittenweem, are now used by fishermen and for leisure craft. Like Culross, the character of the buildings fronting the harbour, shoreline and centre of each small town (they are never far away from the rural hinterland) is mainly of 16th–18th-century date. At Crail, 17th-century cottages hug the steep Shoregate descending to the harbour.

Barrel-vaulted Painted Chamber in the west block of The Palace, executed about 1597. The panels, painted on wood, depict moralising themes, each with appropriate two-line quotation from Geoffrey Whitney's Choice of Emblems published just over a decade earlier, in 1583. (Harvey Wood, National Trust for Scotland).

The wide Marketgate opening out of the main streets above the shore was once one of the largest medieval market places in Europe, now lined with houses dating from the 17th century onwards. The wealth of the fertile rural hinterland, besides maritime trade, brought prosperity, the former immortalised by one resident in a carved inscription reading 'God's blessing is my land and rent'.

Langskaill, Gairsay, Orkney: the enclosing wall and archway from the sea (Rendall).

SHETLAND AND ORKNEY

Both Shetland and Orkney have been mercantile centres and have their own types of merchant houses. *Lodberries* are the traditional form of waterfront house in Lerwick on Shetland. The name is derived from *flat rock*, subsequently replaced by a small private pier from which to unload. Though some of the piers have gone, there are still lodberries in **Lerwick**, those surviving apparently of the early 18th century although they probably occupy much earlier sites. Houses, warehouses and piers also crowd the waterfront of the harbour at **Stromness** on Orkney.

The courtyard remained a feature of Orkney laird/merchant houses throughout the 17th century. The more substantial dwellings lack the verticality of the post-Reformation tower-house, probably impracticable in the windy conditions that prevail and because the islands enjoyed the natural defence of the sea. Of these, Langskaill House, Gairsay, Skaill House, Sandwick, Mainland and Tankerness House, Kirkwall are good examples within a rich heritage.

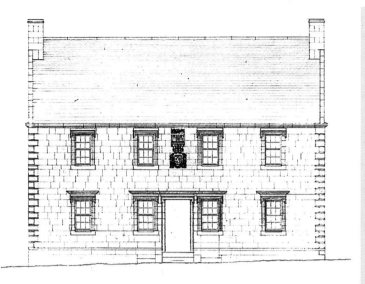

THE BEGINNINGS OF THE FASHION FOR SYMMETRY

A few late 17th-century rural houses emulate the verticality of the tower-house yet enjoy new and innovative regularity of design. This **regularity** properly belongs, in the lesser Scottish house, to the 18th century: yet a certain degree of symmetry, in both plan and elevation, can be observed in some 17th-century lairds' houses.

From now on the **architect**, rarely heard of before 1700 and not established as a profession until the 1830s, takes over the country mansion, and *the country house* passes from traditional building to the domain of conscious architectural design and into an elevated realm beyond the scope of this book.

The stylistic transition from tower-house to merchant house, slowly influenced by fashionable symmetry, occurred over a century or so. By the 18th century, as we will see in the next chapter, the convention of the regular facade became a permanent part of Scottish building tradition.

Master mason's homes

Houses built by master masons as their own homes form a fascinating group. Most masons gained experience and expertise by working on the great mansions of their day. Many filled the role now allocated to the architect, drawing up plans and specifications, but few achieved sufficient prominence for their names to creep into written records. One exception was Tobias Bachop (d.1710), a member of a family of skilled masons from Alloa, who worked extensively for Sir William Bruce, the pioneer of Scottish classicism. Bachop's house, left (1695), has a well-proportioned two-storey ashlar facade revealing an intelligent under-standing of the new symmetrical style architecture. The frontage is embellished with an exquisitely carved mural sundial bearing the date, his initials and those of his wife.
Bachop's House, 25 Kirkgate, Alloa, Clackmannanshire (Clackmannanshire Council).

TRANSITION AND CHANGE

FASHION AND THE

VERNACULAR FROM THE

1700s

W e have seen the transition from vertical tower-house to vernacular merchant house, which gradually assimilated symmetrical features. Now we come, in the 18th century, to the overall acceptance of the regular – fronted house in Scotland for manse, farm house, cottage, all these varying in size according to the status and means of the owner/builder.

OPPOSITE: *Scotsburn House, c.1810, Ross-shire, with regular five-window frontage.*

The 17th-century expansion in trade and communication was to continue throughout the 18th century and beyond; there were improvements and changes in farming, industrial growth and new roads and bridges. Those who prospered built new and more fashionable homes. Some merchants (such as William Forbes in Chapter 4) chose still to build their prosperous new homes in tower-house form, but this was becoming old-fashioned, and we have seen (Chapter 5) how merchant houses of the late 17th century had begun to express, in the regularity of their window pattern and the occasional central ground floor entrance, the influence of the incoming 18th-century fashion of the **symmetrical facade**. This regularity was still often combined with baronial

Amisfield Castle, drawn by Francis Grosse in 1789, by which time the old tower was superseded by the new mansion (Royal Commission on the Ancient and Historical Monuments of Scotland).

characteristics popular in the 16th and 17th centuries. There might be an extruding stair tower or an angle bartizan, the former housing a wheel-stair which was still in use until the later 18th century, while the latter served as a vantage point over the street or landscape rather than as a defence against marauders.

The master mason Tobias Bachop was ahead of his time in 1695 in expressing the new regularity in the modestly sized, though richly detailed house which we have seen he designed and built for himself in Alloa. Similarly, in **Elgin**, **Linlithgow** and elsewhere, symmetrical windows to light the living quarters began to be favoured by those late 17th-century merchants whose homes were above the ground-floor arcaded premises which they used for their trade.

THE ESTABLISHMENT OF SYMMETRY

The change from the conservatism of the 17th century to the symmetry of the 18th percolated throughout house styles. **Pattern books**, including John Reid's *The Scots Gard'ner*, first published in 1683, were influential. So probably were the building works undertaken by engineers of the Ordnance Department who brought English architectural fashion with them when constructing quarters to accompany fortifications, 'built very low, but uniform' in Inverness, Ayr and elsewhere.

So from the turn of the 1700s, medium-sized, regularly-fronted houses began to appear in town and country, to become the backbone of Scottish domestic architectural tradition. These buildings are plainly oblong, but with **symmetrical fenestration**, the windows being rather small and often narrow; they have a central

Balnaguard Inn, Little Dunkeld, Perth, a late 18th century regular-fronted house (Historic Scotland).

doorway and usually gable-end chimney stacks: the piended (hipped) roof continued to find favour in the west. This type served as farmhouse, laird's house or manse: they line the streets of smaller towns and villages, and in single-storey form were subsequently adapted as croft, fisherhouse and farm cottage. This versatile pattern could be enlarged or reduced in size as the means of the patron/builder allowed. Indeed it could be quite imposing as a three-storey, five-bay house, sometimes modest with two storeys or just a cottage in single-storey form. Internal accommodation could be increased where the plan was *double pile* (two rooms deep).

The form was still in general use in the early 20th century as a cottage with central entrance, often heightened to accommodate more generous attic space lit by dormer windows. However, at this less affluent level, there are regional variations dictated by the availability of materials and by local needs and traditions.

LOCAL VARIANTS OF THE SYMMETRICAL THEME

The Shetland Islands are sited in the centre of maritime routes between Scandinavia and Scotland and their 18th-century trading and fishing successes gave rise to a fine series of *haa houses,* two-and three-storey symmetrical dwellings. The moulded and possibly cornised doorway with armorial above is often the sole decorative feature in an otherwise plain front. They are in striking contrast with the low croft houses and the ubiquitous bungalows which otherwise dominate the built landscape.

Haa of Sand, 1754; a Shetland merchant/ laird's house; the small second-floor windows light the attic rooms (Finnie).

Double pile crow-stepped M-gable, Flowerdale, Wester Ross, 1738 (Beaton).

Wester Ross has fine 18th-century lairds' houses associated with the various branches of the Mackenzie family. Of these **Flowerdale**, Gairloch, 1738, and contemporary Applecross House are double-pile mansions of two and three storeys high respectively, with distinctive crowstepped M-gables peculiar to the area. Unusually, Flowerdale has a six-bay frontage, the middle two bays slightly advanced and rising as a central *nepus* gable with apex chimney; the main doorway is squeezed between two windows. At **Applecross** the principal entrance is at the rear (north) while the staircase abuts the central front (south) wall, expressed in the five-window frontage by off-set windows lighting half landings. Flowerdale and Applecross are the only examples of these double-pile, M-gabled mansions in the locality, probably based on Eddercalda or Calda House, a ruinous mansion on the shores of Loch Assynt, Sutherland, built by Kenneth Mackenzie of Assynt around 1725. In turn his mason, probably William MacNeill from Cromarty, took as his model the similarly M-gabled double-pile **Bernera** military barracks at Glenelg, built 1717–1723 to command the Kylerhea crossing to Skye. Here we have another example of the influence on local building traditions of military engineers and architects, whose innovatory practices, like their local workers and the inhabitants of the serrated west coast, communicated and travelled by sea. Another house, built in 1745 at **Udrigle** also on the Gairloch, is a simple two-storey house which, like Applecross, has the stairwell against the front wall and the entrance to the rear, sheltered by a simple porch added in 1756. Though small and plain, consisting only of two rooms on each floor, the principal rooms in the upper storey are remarkable for their panelled walls, box beds and parlour marriage stone, inscribed 'W MC 1745 I MK'. The W stands for William Mackenzie, one of the immensely large and complex family of Mackenzie of Gruinard, Wester Ross.

These west coast houses, all built by land-owning members of the same family within two decades, show the range of possible local adaptions of the 18th-century laird's house.

ROOFS AND GABLES: VARIATIONS ON THE NEW SYMMETRY

The **steeply pitched roofs**, associated with the turn of the 1700s, survived into the first quarter of the 18th century, in part because of the high rainfall of those years, especially in coastal areas. The pronounced sloping surface, particularly when roofed with heavy stone slates, not always lying perfectly flush to each other, speeded the run-off of rainwater. But this steepness of the upper portion of the building is also associated with the tall, vertical lines characteristic of the preceding century.

Watten Mains, Caithness, 1763, with nepus gable and later dormers.

Crowstepped gables lingered on, flat skews coming into general use later in the century, earlier if desired by a wealthy patron who could pay the transport from quarry and masons to prepare and dress the stone. Like crowsteps, they overlaid and protected the vulnerable gablehead to which they clamped the slates. Where there was money to spend on such a refinement, the flat skews project a little to throw surplus water away from the gable; discreet moulding on the underside is a detail always worth looking for.

Another feature that enhances these plain, regularly-fronted houses is the *nepus* or *tympan gable*. This is a central attic gablet rising from the front wallhead with a window or pair of windows, usually an apex chimney stack, which also serves as a finial, and often scroll skewputs. This feature gives the impression of additional height, enhances and dignifies the building and exploits attic space. Depending on the materials, the gablet is semi-circular or simply triangular, the latter more practicable where the local stone is hard to work, such as whinstone or granite; shaping the curved wallhead is difficult with these intractable materials.

Besides Aberdeenshire and Caithness, **nepus gables** are common in Ayrshire, with many local variations. Some are complete with windows and skewputts, most terminate with chimneystacks. Some are in the form of shallow wallhead pediments as though aspiring to classical and conscious architectural design, but in other respects incorporating vernacular features.

There is a fine mid-18th-century three-storey example in The Square, **Huntly**, Aberdeenshire, with central arched pend and semi-circular wallhead gable, austerely constructed in local grey granite, too hard to permit any carved decorative detail. In West

Variations on the theme of nepus-gabled houses are also evident in their materials; for instance in Portsoy, a small trading port on the Banffshire coast, there is peculiar local red harl made with crushed local red stone, a near geological relative to the local serpentine or Portsoy Marble. A fine example stands in North High Street (No. 23/27), a seafaring captain or merchant's house of around 1730, with a central gable enhanced by a round-headed, key-stoned window.

Glazing

The grace and dignity of these houses is further enhanced by the glazing. Eighteenth-century crown glass was manufactured in large circular discs. The red-hot molten material on the end of a blowing-iron was spun round and round, then beaten flat by the glass blower to result in a disc up to 4ft 6in (1.36m) in diameter: the central thick 'bull's eye' or knob was discarded. The resulting panes often have a slightly wavy surface and glint, delicately enlivening the windows and the entire facade. In Scotland, the 19th-century lying-pane or 'landskip' glazing (below) was fashion-able, continuing in the Highlands as late as the 1880s when it had died out elsewhere.

Lying pane

Anstruther one of the houses lining the High Street Street has its wallhead *nepus* gablet rising above its neighbours in order to view the sea and harbour. These little rooms are the direct successors of the small caphouse chambers corbelled out above circular stairwells in earlier tower-houses, similar to the *Outlook Tower chamber* in The Study, **Culross** (*c.*1610) overlooking the marine highway of the Firth of Forth.

DOORS AND WINDOWS AND THEIR GLAZING

The most important features, enlivening the otherwise austere frontage of the standard 18th-century lairds's house and farmhouse, are the main **doorway** and **fenestration**. The window pattern, particularly the glazing of those windows, coupled with the principal entrance, are the only features to give either decoration or pretension (or lack of it) to the house.

Most doorways were moulded, either simple *chamfer* or something more complex. A popular detail was the extension of the **moulded lintel** as eared or *lugged* architraves, returning each side of the opening. Armorials or datestones combining monograms or initials are sited above the main entrance.

Doors were wooden and panelled. Local house carpenters had their own style and decorative detailing. It is always a rewarding experience to examine the main doors and wooden architraves of the surviving examples of this period; so often they reflect a local joiner's skill, with raised panelling, beading and exploitation of the grain of the wood. Doorways were further enhanced by **fanlights** with radial glazing which illuminated the entrance hall within.

Though the greater mansions boasted large windows, in these lesser dwellings they tended to be smaller and narrower in the first half of the century. Not only did these smaller windows have the advantage of being cheaper in their use of glass but also structurally they saved piercing large voids in the masonry, which had the consequence of weakening the walling. If it was desired that the front rooms be more generously lit, then the five-windowed front allowed two windows to each of the main outer rooms and a single one to light the central stairwell. It was attractively fashionable around 1730–1740 to pair these outer windows and sometimes to accentuate the central first-floor light by giving it a curved lintel and intersecting glazing to the upper sash. This very simple detail enhances an otherwise plain frontage and was the modest counterpart of the grandiose first-floor Venetian window, an 18th-

LEFT:
Anstruther doorpiece, 1718; intricate moulding and carving give stature to an otherwise plain house (Beaton).

RIGHT:
Corniced doorpiece, Banff, 1740, fronting a plain house said to have belonged to a silversmith (Beaton).

LEFT:
Pediment and 'lugged' surround, Shewglie, Inverness-shire, 1762 (Beaton).

RIGHT:
Classical detailing, Portsoy, Banffshire (Beaton).

The Arched House, Ecclefechan, Dumfriesshire, 1790. Built by stonemason brothers named Carlyle, with a house for each and central arched entrance to rear area and workplace. The small paired windows above the arch add grace to the building, which is otherwise unadorned (National Trust for Scotland).

century fashionable attribute to the greater house. This window type was adapted by the Carlyle brothers for their adjacent houses around 1790.

Taller windows in the first floor express the location within the house of the main public rooms, for the continental *piano nobile,* with parlour in the first floor, was traditional in Scotland well into the 19th century. Where there are three storeys, the second-floor windows are usually smaller, the same width as those below, but shorter, contributing to the vertical pattern of the facade and expressing the secondary nature of the accommodation on the top floor. By the 18th century, the sliding sash-and-case window was well established in these houses, multi-pane glazing making a neat and positive contribution to the frontage, particularly where the *astragals* (glazing bars) are painted a pale colour. Astragals tended to be broad in the early 1800s becoming finer as the century wore on.

STAIRCASES

The traditional stone **wheel**-or **turnpike stair** that corkscrewed within wall thickness or turrets in medieval castles and post-Reformation tower-houses survived well into the 18th century. Stair towers abutted the plain frontage of a house in the 17th century, housing turn-pikes that served each floor. In the 18th century these tended to be at the rear providing more space within houses (and serving flatted dwellings in towns). The wheel-stair, however, was also accommodated inside the fashionable regular-fronted house in a central circular stairwell. Wooden staircase, with silhouette or turned balusters were popular where timber was plentiful; decorative cast-iron balusters were fashionable from the late 18th century onwards.

In 18th-century houses there is much overlap in staircase types; models which were old-fashioned, such as the stone wheel-stair, remained practical (they never wear out!) and popular well on in the 1700s. The skills of constructing such stairs, of making their triangular treads and fitting one on top of the other, survived beyond the castle and tower-house period when they had been a standard fitting.

However, it is not only stairs that are difficult to fit into a neat chronological pattern when discussing the improved landowner, merchant or affluent farmer's home of the 18th century. Traditions died hard, success came and went at different times in different places, some changes were slow to establish themselves. This infinite variety offers endless fascination.

Wheel-stair (Beaton).

Roderick McDonald's Inn in Ross-shire drawn by Moses Griffith for Thomas Pennant, who toured Scotland in 1769. This is an example of the cruck-framed turf building lived in at the same time, and sometimes in the same location, as the symmetrical masonry dwellings outlined in this chapter. (National Galleries of Scotland).

Fashionable symmetry was adapted for manses and good farm houses right down the social scale to the single storey cottage. However, it is important to remember that alternative vernacular traditions which we looked at in earlier chapters continued to exist in parallel: some bonnet lairds, farmers and ministers still resided in cruck-framed longhouses or creel-houses.

CHAPTER 7

PLANNING AND IMPROVEMENT

HOMES FOR WORKERS

This chapter looks at the range of housing developed in the 18th–19th centuries in response to changes in farming, the movement of increasing numbers of the rural population to new planned towns, the effects of industry and the expanding network of communications by road, rail and canal.

The rationalisation and **improvements** in agriculture which commenced in the later 18th century brought about the re-organisation of farms and their buildings. The farming landscape, as we see it today, dates largely from these improvements, with **enclosure** of fields with dry-stone dykes or thorn hedges, stone farmhouses and sturdy steadings. The enclosure of fields necessitated the relocation of small subsistence tenants; this was either to new settlements – the *planned towns*, initiated and partly financed by the landowner – or to cottages associated with the farms where they then became employees. Landowners expanded their estate buildings and improved their policies, enclosing them with walls for privacy and providing access through a driveway, whose gates required a gatekeeper, who in turn needed accommodation. New farmhouses and steadings were followed by farm workers' cottages (usually in that order), now standing a little distance from the steading and main house. The development of **communications** from the mid-18th century onwards - the making of roads, the bridging of rivers and the construction of canals and railways, forging through the countryside - brought workers requiring accommodation for their families. Money to pay for the new roads and bridges was raised by

OPPOSITE:
*Farm cottages,
Carskiey Farm,
Southend, Argyll
(Montgomery).*

tolls, so the toll-keeper had to be housed as did canal and railway workers. Many large industrial units had their beginnings in **rural industries** such as weaving. Most spinning and weaving was carried out at home, in villages and small towns, progressing to small domestic units before expanding in industrial premises as technology developed, the location in due course frequently engulfed by urban growth.

FARM COTTAGES

Farm workers' cottages as a recognisable type provided by the landowner only date from the **improved** farming era. Before then labourers lived in poor houses or *cots*, mean huts of turf, probably without a window, and with a hurdle door. They were often in

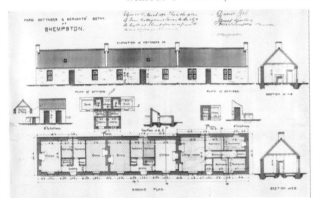

settlements or *cottowns* which were also the homes of thatchers, carters, ditchers and so on. Robert Thomson (in Chapter 1) described the stone and turf houses of his father's cottars in Aberdeenshire whose 'tiny hamlet presented somewhat the appearance of huge bee-hives...without the least attempt at order or effect'.

Improved farm workers' cottages and servants' bothy, Shempston, Moray, designed by Reid and Wittet, Elgin, 1895. Two two-roomed cottages for married farm workers and a bothy for single workers with four rooms and kitchen. The latter was luxurious compared with most others. The range was served by outside privies and ashpits (ash from fires re-used as ground fertiliser): there was a pigsty with yard for each cottage (Falconer).

Around 1800 they were 'a partial survival of a system of land-tenure once very common in Scotland [working as required] upon the farm and depending [on his father] for a great part of their daily bread'. In 1798 the farm of Meikle Tarrel, **Tarbat**, Easter Ross came into the hands of an innovative farmer who had studied the most improved system of agriculture in East Lothian. He found the farm 'occupied by several small tenants whose lands were in a state of wretchedness, and their houses afforded accommodation for neither man nor beast'.

There are obviously local variations of time-scale, but for the most part improved farm cottages date from the 1840s onwards. They were small, usually of just two rooms, with rubble walls, mural hearths and thatched, pantiled or slated roofs. As time went on, accommodation increased with additional rooms or the loft dormered to provide upstairs space. Much later a rear wing made room for a working kitchen and bathroom with flush toilet.

Cottages were for the most part for workers with families: the housing of the single men was less good. There was always a turnover of the single labourer, who changed farms every six months at the *feeing* markets (his married counterpart followed suit annually), usually within a 20-mile radius. Accommodation was in bothies, a room in the steading or separate building where men slept and cooked for themselves. At Glamis Mains, Angus, the unmarried men had two rooms in one wing of the steading. Here the ground-floor room had a hearth and was used for cooking and living; a grill in the ceiling allowed the heat from the fire to filter upwards to the sleeping room above. This was a large farm on a wealthy estate which could well afford such (comparative) luxury. In north-east and west central Scotland the *kitchie* system prevailed; the men slept in a room above or near their horses, but ate in the farmhouse kitchen. These rooms were *chaumers* in the north-east and *berricks* (barracks) in Moray.

PLANNED TOWNS

As runrig cottowns were phased out with field enclosure and rationalisation of the larger farms, some of the surplus population found homes in the newly planned settlements established from the mid-18th century onwards. These **planned towns** were, despite the urban sounding nomenclature, more village than town. They very

Bowmore, Isla, Argyll, a planned village established in 1768: the main street runs from the jetty on Loch Idaal to the church, lined with plain, mainly two-storey whitewashed houses. The vista is closed by the round church, gifted by the landowner, Daniel Campbell who built it 'at his own charges and dedicated it to the Supreme Deity in the year 1769' (Historic Scotland).

NEWTON STEWART: a planned town

The Imperial Gazetteer of Scotland (c.1858) reports that Newton Stewart, Wigtownshire, was established as early as 1701 at 'a convenient stage between Ferry-town-of-Cree and Glenluce, and a suitable depot and resort for an extensive tract of circumjacent country'. Though 'Smuggling did something to promote its advancement' more legitimate wealth was generated by 'a decent inn or two, a few shops, and some work rooms for ordinary artisans'. Newton Stewart, with its low-key, white-harled houses lining streets winding along the banks of the River Cree, still serves as a local centre and is popular with tourists.

often exploited poor ground. **Grantown-on-Spey**, laid out on a barren moor in 1765–1766, soon generated income from *feus* (ground rents) from land previously worthless. Others straddled main highways where the new village inn offered shelter and nourishment for both traveller and horse; they were the location for markets, for local services such as smithy and shoemaker and for new sources of work, particularly in textile-related industries. They benefited from the improvement of roads and construction of bridges which took place in the hundred years from 1730 to 1830.

The **layout** of these villages was formal; grid-iron, cruciform or a long single street. Housing, at least in the centre of the larger settlements, was usually two-storey; there could be building specification as at **Kingussie**, Inverness-shire (c.1790) where cottages were to have masonry rather than clay walls. Houses opened directly to the street, for it was thought that residents would use frontage space as a *midden* for rubbish. Most had plots of land at the rear for cultivation of vegetables or maintenance of a cow; sometimes arable land or grazing was also available. Some villages were more prestigious than others; where the landlord was generously paternalistic or wished to create a good impression (or both) he would provide schools, church and other public buildings. For instance, both **Fochabers**, Moray and **Cullen**, Banffshire replaced settlements within the landowners policies, respectively the Dukes of Gordon and the Earls of Seafield. Besides their proximity to the estate, both new villages straddled main highways; the well planned streets lined with neat rows of houses, and central square created a good impression on those passing through. The Kirkton of Old Cullen was uncomfortably close to **Cullen** House: the new village was laid out between 1819 and 1820, nearer the *seatown*, by a local surveyor George MacWilliam, the houses fronting The Square and principal streets designed by William Robertson, an Elgin architect. **Inveraray** on the shores of Loch Fyne, is architecturally the finest of them all, initiated by Archibald, 3rd Duke of Argyll, in 1744 but not completed until the end of the century by the 5th Duke who succeeded in 1770. The neat rows of white-harled two- and three-storey flatted dwellings are of a traditional nature, the manse and other better houses enhanced with architectural embellishment, the town aggrandised by John Adam's hotel (1751–1755) and as a centrepiece, there are the dual Gaelic and English churches designed by Robert Mylne, 1795–1800.

The provision of public buildings by the landlord varied. At Fochabers the Duke of Gordon paid for the parish church, designed by John Baxter of Edinburgh, 1798, together with the flanking manse and combined townhall and school, while at Cullen the Earl of Seafield constructed a range fronting the central square comprising townhall, 'commodious courthouse', post office, hotel and even a ballroom. Some new villages foundered, either because there was no local employment or the industries established by the landlord failed. Once the railway was introduced there was no demand for these settlements, for the farm produce could be easily transported to the urban areas where many country people moved for work.

THE HOME AS THE WORKPLACE: WEAVERS' HOUSING

Before **textile industries** became mechanised and industrialised, often engulfed in urban sprawl, they were largely rural enterprises, established where the raw materials were available, water power plentiful, sea or canal transport near at hand or encouraged as a way of livelihood for residents of newly established planned towns. Some textile processing, such as weaving, operated from home in small country towns and villages. Linen weaving, from locally grown flax, was an important industry in Angus and Perthshire, largely carried on either in the ground floor of the home or in the attic floor where the looms exploited the roof space. Ground floor workrooms were more satisfactory, in part because of greater light and also because earth floors were practical for damp thread, which kept supple if moist. Some of these linen weavers' homes were two-storey, the windows in the ground floor larger to give additional light to the looms while the domestic quarters, including the kitchen, were upstairs.

Linen hand-loom weaver's cottage, Kilbarchan, Renfrew. The door lintel is inscribed 'BUILDED ANNO 1723 BY ANDREW BRYDEIN JENAT BRYDEIN'. A split level cottage which is part dwelling and part workshop. From small beginnings, Kilbarchan expanded as a weaving centre; at the peak of activity every cottage had a loom, with over 600 in the village (National Trust for Scotland).

The home was also the workplace for **cotton hand-loom weavers**, centred largely in Ayrshire (Crosshill and Kirkmichael) and Lanarkshire (Stonehouse). Robert Brown of Newhall founded **Carlops**, Peebleshire, in 1784 as a cotton weavers' village, the same year as **New Lanark** was established by David Dale and Richard Arkwright. Though (originally) in a rural setting, New Lanark workers lived in flatted accommodation reminiscent of urban dwellings while industrialised weaving was carried on in mills. This worker housing was unusual for its time; other cotton mill centres are notable for rows of single two-storey workers' dwellings.

INDUSTRIAL HOUSING

In stark contrast to linen weaving in fertile Angus and lowland Perthshire, the **lead mining** at Wanlockhead and Leadhills, on the Dumfriesshire/Lanarkshire borders was sited on high ground 'of the most sterile description'. The sole residents were the miners living in simple cottages similar to other rural dwellings. In **Wanlockhead** these had been rebuilt around 1720 and again after 1842 after change of ownership. By the mid-19th century the population was around 800 in each village, by which time the lead mining activities had reached their peak.

Wanlockhead leadmines, c.1775 (Royal Commission on the Ancient and Historical Monuments of Scotland).

There were also lead mines at **Strontian**, north Argyll, where the 'village was at one time a filthy clachan; but in 1828 under the

direction of Sir James Riddell [landowner] and his lady, it underwent a total revolution; and it now [c.1858] consists partly of neat new slated cottages, and partly of renovated old huts.'

Coal and iron **mining**, carried on since medieval times, started in rural areas, which became urbanised with an expanding population. **Brick**, not widespread in Scotland for house building, makes an unexpected appearance; the fireclay used a by-product of mining activity (see Chapter 1). The village of **Rosewell**, Midlothian, had a population of 390 in 1861; 30 years later this had almost quadrupled to 1394, accounting for the neat rows of miners' brick cottages (*miners' raws*) in Victoria and Lothian Streets, the building material

from the nearby Whitehill brickworks. These cottages are of traditional two/three-room type, and except that there are so many of them, similar to many country estate or farm cottages. As in other industrial areas of Great Britain, rows of cottages and houses are a familiar sight in mining villages and towns of Scotland, the housing standards improving from the late 19th century onwards.

'Miners' raws': brick-built coalminers' cottages, Rosewell, Midlothian (Royal Commission on the Ancient and Historical Monuments of Scotland).

The most northerly coal mines in Scotland (producing coal until the mid-20th century) were at **Brora**, Sutherland, where the Marquis of Stafford and Countess of Sutherland (from 1833 Duke and Duchess of Sutherland) also established brick works. The Terrace, Victoria Street, 1875, is a handsome row of two-storey and attic houses, built for workers in the various Sutherland enterprises in Brora. Though the brick walling is unusual in Sutherland, the tooled stone dressings, dormers, *barge-boards* and chimney stacks are

In Sutherland, the well known English country house architect, George Devey, exponent of the vernacular revival, designed buildings for the second Duke of Sutherland in the late 1850s, initiating an unmistakable Sutherland estate pattern. Devey's work was executed by the estate Surveyor, William Fowler, who thereafter drew on Devey's local work and style: deep eaves supported by corbelled gable brackets, tall chimneys, characteristic dormers, generous windows. Larger and smaller versions of this architectural tradition, cottages, houses, inns, shooting lodges and schools, abound throughout the entire county, all with local stone for masonry, instantly recognisable, usually dated and often identified with a large S.

unmistakably drawn from the estate architectural vocabulary described below.

ESTATE HOUSING AND TRADITIONS

As with the countryside, so rural estates were also subject to change. Gracious parks studded with large trees became fashionable, enclosed with walls and entered by a driveway through imposing gates.

Dwelling houses are just a part of the wide range of buildings found on country estates: dovecots, stables, laundries, *Mains farms* (home farms) all play their part in large rural properties which were institutions and communities within themselves, large employers of labour and often depositories of excellent construction skills. Estate housing frequently followed an individual **estate style** creating a local tradition: *barge-boards* (wooden boards edging gables) could be intricately carved in a particular pattern; windows and dormers might be of a local type; masonry and roofing came from the estate quarries; the housing of employees reflected the concern or otherwise of the estate owner and his factor. In general, surviving estate houses and cottages are of 19th- and early 20th-century date, though particular buildings can be earlier or later.

Some estates were innovative with their buildings. Samuel Barham, an Englishman, was appointed Master of Works on the Ardtornish Estate, in northern Argyll, in 1870. From 1871 the buildings he designed there were executed in concrete. All differed a little one from the other, all enjoyed picturesque designs, high gables, decorative barge-boards and well-proportioned windows and doors. While his predecessor had also used some of this vocabulary, probably drawn from pattern books, Barham's work was sensitive rather than solid, delightful in its exploitation of site and resulting in attractive architectural compositions. The estate cottages designed by Barham cost about £200 each, containing six rooms and some with indoor water closets, a remarkable convenience for workers' housing in the 1870s.

Gate-lodges

The **gate-lodge** is intended to shelter the man (and his family) responsible for opening and shutting the gates separating the mansion house from the main thoroughfare, a practice dating mainly from the 18th century onwards. This coincides with both the formal landscaping of policies through which the admiring visitor would progress and the development of roads, which earlier (and indeed later) were tracks, with ever increasing traffic including droved beasts to cattle fairs. The lodge can therefore be later than the mansion but, if built contemporarily with the principal house, it could anticipate and reflect in miniature the grandeur ahead.

Gate-lodge accommodation could be, and usually was, minimal until well into the 19th century. Architectural design or idiosyncratic form often took precedence over internal convenience. Oval, round, polygonal or square boxes made quaint and picturesque additions to the main gate: never mind about accommodating the wife and children! Lodges always had windows overlooking road and driveway in order to anticipate the arrival of family and visitors. Sometimes they were in pairs, linked by a grand entrance or archway: the practical issue here was that there was always a relief keeper on hand. From the mid-19th century, the lodge took on more generous proportions, usually of two storeys, even if masked within a baronial or classical revival shell.

Octagonal early 19th-century gate-lodge, Armadale, Skye (Beaton).

TOLLHOUSES AND DWELLINGS ASSOCIATED WITH TRANSPORT

Tollhouses on roads and bridges (*pontage houses: pont* = bridge) were strategically sited for the collection of dues to recuperate construction and maintenance costs. They are a familiar sight, usually small, distinctly shaped, and not unlike gate-lodges; most were

Tollhouse, Monymusk, Aberdeenshire. Local granite rubble and slates. The bow-fronted projection is common in Aberdeenshire, with windows overlooking the road (Beaton).

Arbroath Signal Tower constructed in 1813, to plans drawn by Robert Stevenson, to communicate with the Bell Rock Lighthouse 11.5 miles (18.5km) offshore, incorporating living quarters for the lightkeepers' families. If a baby was born to a keeper's wife while he was on duty in the lighthouse, a pair of breeks for a boy or a dress for a girl would be hoisted on the signal mast, the happy news observed by telescope (Angus Council).

consciously designed. **Toll-keepers** had to keep a look out, so again windows were placed each side of the cottage in order that both approaches were visible from indoors. *Tollhouses* are largely of 19th-century date coinciding with the great age of road improvement and bridge building in Scotland.

Lock-keepers on the Crinan and Caledonian canals, respectively opened in 1809 and 1822, required cottages: their place of duty was often isolated and they were on call almost permanently. More isolated were **lighthouse-keepers** on lonely headlands or distant islands. Where families accompanied the keepers, housing was incorporated within the complex. For a century the dynasty of Stevenson family engineers designed lighthouses and lightkeepers' dwellings for the Commission for Northern Lights: the cottages are grouped in linear formation, usually fronting the lighthouse and enclosed within a walled court. Many have flat roofs and handsome pilastered Egyptian-style frontages creating a Scottish lighthouse tradition of its own; others are flatted, double-pile dwellings.

The **railway network** in Scotland started in earnest in the 1830s, reaching Wick and Thurso in the the far north by 1874 and penetrating along the west coast to Mallaig in 1901. Station master's accommodation was frequently incorporated above the main station building, with linesmen's and signalmen's cottages nearby. Stylistically these vary from Scottish traditional masonry buildings, obviously adapted for railway use, to the turn of the century, white-washed cottages on the west coast line between **Oban** and **Mallaig**. Small, often brick-built bothies, stand along the lines, to shelter those working on or checking the track. For these the brick was brought on site by train. Railway lines had their own styles which are as recognisable to railway building enthusiasts as engines to train spotters! Of note are those between **Golspie** and **Helmsdale**, for the Duke of Sutherland was entirely responsible for the construction of this stretch between 1868 and 1871: the buildings were designed in the estate office by William Fowler and are stylistically similar to Sutherland estate shooting lodges, farmhouses and cottages of the period.

Lock-keeper's house, Crinan Canal (Montgomery).

We have seen how *improved* farming changed not only the landscape but the housing of country people, necessitating either farm cottages or new villages to house those removed from the land. New industries and communication required workers for whom housing had to be provided. Country estates developed their own estate style housing for employees. Throughout the developments the hand of the improver, landowner or industrialist can be seen shaping the ongoing vernacular.

CHAPTER 8

FISHER COTTAGES AND FISHERTOWNS

S cotland is a country almost surrounded by sea. In this chapter we look at the homes of those for whom it has provided a livelihood.

The harvest of the sea has been gathered from off Scotland's shores from the earliest times and on something approaching an industrial scale from at least the medieval period. Although most of our surviving fishertowns are of 18th-century or later origins, a few are earlier: **Auchmithie** in Angus (illustrated on page 46), supplied fish to Arbroath Abbey to which it belonged. Once it became possible to cure fish for preservation in quantity, markets at home and abroad expanded, sea fishing became a way of life and fisher-folk, by the nature of their life style, formed small, close-knit coastal communities wherever there was sufficient shelter.

Groups of small cottages, similar to their rural counterparts, built of stone or clay, with thatched, pantiled or slated roofs, huddled randomly by the shore. If shore-side siting was impossible, houses were situated on the cliffs above – burdening the fisherfolk, both men and women, with steep climbs carrying catch, lines, nets, bait and boat gear. Local fish sales were carried on by the women, who travelled to nearby towns and many miles in the surrounding countryside carrying heavy creels of fish for sale or to barter for rural produce such as eggs, butter, cheese, etc.

Early fisher dwellings were small, even mean: they were also the workplace, for baiting, line preparation and storage of gear. Improvement in housing and aspirations for greater space and comfort had little fixed timescale; it depended more on the prosperity of the fishing in any one location. There are variations of house plan and type, developed in part by the physical nature of the

OPPOSITE: *Congested housing in the fishertown of Sandend, Banffshire (Beaton).*

site and in part by the demands of fishing. In the late 20th century the home is no longer the workplace, for large, modern boats require deep-water harbourage seldom available in their village of origin, from where the fishermen commute by car to their boats.

BANFFSHIRE SEATOWNS

Seatowns on the Banffshire coast reveal the chronological development of the **fisher houses** and make a useful case-study from which parallels and differences with other areas can be drawn. Eighteenth-century estate maps record cottages at **Cullen** Seatown scattered along the crescent-shaped shoreline of Cullen Bay and the random nature of the housing pattern is still clearly evident. Low, clay and boulder cottages, thatched roofs, now replaced with pantiles or slate, are the earliest type. These were two-roomed cottages, with earth or clay floors scrubbed and sanded after line baiting had been completed; cement floors covered with linoleum superseded clay. It was the kitchen (*kitchie*) that was living room and bedroom combined, fitted with box beds. The other room (*the Room*) was used for special occasions. The loft was for storage of fishing gear, possibly also a sleeping place for boys. Randomly sited, often with only a slip of a passage between, known as the *gless hole*, with room enough to clean or replace windowpanes. Double-leaf plank doors were usual in the earlier cottages.

As elsewhere, these single-storey cottages were raised at the wallhead when times prospered and means became available for desirable additional space; houses were too closely packed here and elsewhere to allow sideways extension. Tell-tale changes of masonry indicate where there has been **heightening**.

'Tartan tounie' paintwork (Beaton).

The 1880s coincided with the expansion of fishing communities and the arrival of the coastal railway. Much of the area had a natural shortage of good stone for dressings, door jambs, chimneyheads, window lintels, etc. Portland cement, easily transported by the new railway, arrived by the bagful and was utilized on site to mix **concrete** and cast the necessary masonry finishings in moulds. The standardisation of this concrete masonry is apparent. However, concrete is drab and the practice of painting it soon became general, often in bright colours, earning the Banffshire coastal villages

the sobriquet of 'Tartan Tounies'! Of these, Cullen Seatown, **Findochty** and **Portknockie** display a particular taste for colour, often painting the entire frontage and *stroking* or outlining the mortar courses with fine white paint. The overall effect is felicitous and has slipped easily into the local building tradition. The sale to private owners of local authority housing during the 1980s and 1990s, some of it constructed from rubble masonry with concrete dressings, has generated a new round of house painting.

The population of these Banffshire coast seatowns doubled and trebled during the second half of the 19th century, the new houses built on regular feued plots laid out as straight streets. Houses were either single storey, with attics lit by canted (angled) bay dormers known locally as *bays*, or two storeys high, the upper floor breaking the wallhead with gabled dormers. House carpentry became a feature of these new-style Banffshire fishertown houses, in particular the front door. These were always panelled, a local type had a deep convex rail across the centre while door jambs were pilastered. Where new streets housed more prosperous members of the fishing community – boat owners, fisher merchants and others associated with chandlery or roperies – the doorways were wide with sidelights and overlights illuminating the inner hallway, glazed with *art nouveau* patterned coloured lights and, of course, closed by handsome panelled doors.

Besides the family, homes had to furnish **storage** for fishing gear: the earlier single-storey cottages often had a small single bay extension (now utilised as bathroom or kitchen) with separate entrance; many had hearths (nets and lines had to be boiled in bark as a preservative), the tell-tale small ridge chimney suggesting a *hinging lum*, which could be utilised for drying or smoking fish. Where gear was stored in the **attic**, this had to be carried through

Portknockie, Banffshire: bracketted cornices above doors and long-short jambs are painted concrete, the mortar courses of the rubble masonry frontages are outlined or 'stroked' with white paint. Well carpentered doors and canted wallhead dormers ('bays') are characteristic of this c. 1900 fishertown housing (Beaton).

the house or eased in through a small gabled end window, closed by an inside wooden shutter; this was normal practice as late at the 1930s. The later houses had rear external stairs to reach the loft, which were floored but unlined, for exposed beams were ideal for hanging nets, while equipment was stored in the *crap o' the wa'*, the angle where the slope of roof and floor met.

FISHERTOWNS ELSEWHERE

At **Crovie**, near Fraserburgh in Aberdeenshire, there is but a narrow strip between sea and cliff; cottages, as elsewhere were mostly constructed with their gable ends facing the sea to reduce the effect of wind and spray on the home and with external storm shutters

Crail, Fife; Shoregate, lined with 17th-and 18th-century houses, links the harbour with the town (Beaton).

which could be fastened. There is a peculiar Crovie house type, a single-storey and attic, three-bay cottage built into the hillside above a single-bay ground-floor net store; the living quarters are reached by a forestair. Other fisher villages in the Fraserburgh area such as **Sandhaven** and **Broadsea** had stone projections incorporated in the gable ends on which to hang coiled fisherlines.

Ferryden, Angus is also between hillside and sea, separated from Montrose by the river-mouth. Fisher houses here are two-storey flatted dwellings, with the upper house reached by a forestair oversailing the doorway of the one below. The dwellings vary in size, mostly with centre door and flanking window, but are smaller, squeezing two two-bay flats with paired front doors into the same floor space as the larger apartment above. The siting of Ferryden with regard to Montrose is typical of many fishertowns associated with larger urban centres, nearby but separate. In Ferryden, as in Gardenstown in Aberdeenshire, when a fisherman was successful and became prosperous, he and his family moved to a street further up the hillside – real one-upmanship!

In the 1920s and 1930s local authority houses in **Cellardyke**, Fife, utilising exactly the same designs as in more urban settings, have the modification of access doors high in the gable end of the building over which is a pulley for hauling nets into the shared loft space of two- and three-storey flatted buildings

As with Ferryden and Montrose, Newton-on-Ayr is separated by the river from the county town of Ayr. The settlement is said to have been established by fishers from Pitsligo, Aberdeenshire between 1770 and 1780: they had been press-ganged into the navy in the north-east and released in the Firth of Clyde. **Dunure**, further west along the Ayrshire coast, is a characteristic fishing village with a small, sheltered harbour too small and shallow for contemporary boats. It was established in about 1800, increasing in size to reach around 300 inhabitants a century later. Houses were mainly small single-storey dwellings with two ground floor rooms and a large loft: this was divided in half, part for fishing gear and part as sleeping accommodation for boys, the parents and girls squeezing into the ground floor.

PLANNED FISHERTOWNS

By the 18th century, fish salted and packed in barrels, or dried, was an established exportable commodity. Landlords realised that capital investment in fishing communities could bring returns while the British Fisheries Society was founded in 1786 to promote fishing. This period coincided with the growth of planned towns and villages, a movement influencing coastal settlements as well as the countryside.

Surveyors and architects were involved in new fishing settlements. **Footdee**, at the seaward end of Aberdeen harbour and some distance from the town, was laid out by John Smith, architect, in the early 19th century, as two hollow squares enclosed by cottages; many were later raised to two storeys and the squares partially filled by *tarry sheds*, the fishermen's stores.

10 Shore Street, Inver (Beaton).

At Inver in Easter Ross, the cottages have clay walls, but follow a plan form peculiar to the area with a through passage, passing front to back of the cottage – perhaps to facilitate quick access to the beach. Number 10 Shore Street has three rooms, two intercommunicating while the through passage separates kitchen and bedroom. The kitchen hearth, with hanging chimney, backs against the passage, while the outer rooms have mural fireplaces. These are expressed externally by gable end chimneys, the kitchen hearth served by an off-centre ridge stack.

Tobermory, Mull: sketch of proposed elevation of buildings in the planned fishing settlement c. 1788 (Scottish Record Office).

The unusual west coast Highland fishing settlement of **Corran**, Glenelg, on the north shores of Loch Hourne, Inverness-shire has a linear layout with a difference. A terrace of single storey cottages (there is some later heightening), fronted by small gardens, enjoys a level site overlooking the loch. Behind, at right angles with a running level down the slope, is a row of a dozen rubble, corrugated-iron roofed cow byres, served by a common drainage ditch and lane. By the shore are fishing sheds, again as a continuous terrace and again roofed in corrugated iron. All walling is rubble, the cottages are harled and have slated roofs, piended on the end dwellings in the local tradition (see Chapter 3): the cottages, like the byres and fishing sheds, were probably originally thatched. Here the numerical correlation between cottages, byres and fishing stores indicate that crofting and fishing were dual occupations of the inhabitants. The linear layout was probably dictated by the Dochfour Estate, near Inverness whose laird, James Baillie, purchased Glenelg in 1837 when fish were plentiful in Loch Hourne.

The well known civil engineer, Thomas Telford served the British Fisheries Society as surveyor and advisor for their fishing settlements. The Society was established in 1786 to erect:

'Free Towns, Villages and Fishing Stations in the Highlands and Islands of Scotland as the most effectual means of improving the Fisheries.......and [providing] employment for the Inhabitants at home; and thereby putting a stop to the dangerous spirit of Emigration now prevalent in many parts of that Country'.

New settlements were established on the west coast, at **Tobermory**, **Mull**, **Ullapool**, **Wester Ross** and **Lochbay** (Stein village), **Skye**: unfortunately the herring disappeared soon after these three villages were built in the decade 1788–1798. Tobermory held its own as a commercial and later a tourist centre, Ullapool fared poorly until there was a revival of the fishing and tourism in mid 20th century while Lochbay, the smallest, reverted to crofting like the rest of Skye.

Pulteneytown, **Caithness**, separated from Wick by the Wick River, was a substantial town laid out by Telford, who also designed the first harbour, c.1807–1811. Though the west coast fishing towns had always had some provision for crofting, Pulteneytown was intended only for the fishing industry and thrived as such well into this century, as long as fishing prospered. The core of the town was constructed between 1810–1830, sited on high ground above the river and harbour in a **grid pattern** centred on Argyle Square, the streets named after the directors of the British Fisheries Society: Smith Terrace, Huddart Street, Vansittart Street, etc. Housing is mostly two-storey, opening direct to the roadside with access to rear gardens, in line with contemporary thought that space in front of houses would be used as deposit for waste. The houses were well built of stone with local slate roofs, regular fenestration and doors, the accommodation generous by fisher standards. That they were not all alike was bemoaned by Telford who had drawn up plans, costing about £300 per house, and hoped for 'uniformity of Building in point of Elevation of the Houses and dimensions of the Doors and Windows'. Herring fishing was with nets and on an industrialised scale in Pulteneytown. The houses therefore provided no storage for major fishing gear nor were the kitchens used for baiting lines: these were essentially somewhat different from the standard fisher house.

Corran, Glenelg: linear byres in the foreground with the terrace of white-washed cottages, centre; a row of rubble fishing stores stand by the shores of Loch Hourne, with the hills of Knoydart in the background (Beaton).

In this chapter we have seen how fisher housing varied from place to place and how it improved when fishing prospered. Sadly, in view of their long tradition, many fishertowns are now merely 'dormitories' as the boats require deep water harbourage available only in the larger fisherports.

MAIN ROAD

BEDROOM

3 BEDROOMS
OVER

LIVING ROOM

PANTRY

SCULLERY

WASHOUSE
E.C. AND COAL
UNDER THIS

GATE

PRIVATE ROAD

W.CVRTIS GREEN
1897

LODGE AT SCOULAG
ISLE OF BUTE
R.WEIR SCHULTZ ARCHIT
14 GRAYS INN SQUARE
W.C.

VERNACULAR REVIVAL AND SURVIVAL

As a final note to this review of Scotland's wide heritage of house-types, we will look at the revival of interest in these vernacular building traditions, how they have provided a rich design source for architects and how at the end of the 20th century new roles for the fragile small rural cottage can be identified.

Concurrently with the final stages of indigenous vernacular building in Scotland, architects were looking for new sources of inspiration – and with the revival of interest in Scottish history and culture, the success of Sir Walter Scott's novels and the mid-19th century expansion of the sporting estate, they sought for design sources that would mirror the **Scottishness** of Scotland's buildings.

From the mid-19th century, by which time the architectural profession was established, some looked to the old castles for new ideas. This was the age of the country house, either enlargements and redesigns of earlier buildings for old families, or new mansions. They were often the ambitious projects of wealthy industrial entrepreneurs, in England as well as Scotland, who wished to establish themselves as country landowners. Once the railway network was developed these gentleman and their families could, and did, come to Scotland to indulge in both landownership and sport. Scotland became fashionable, a fashion enthusiastically led by Queen Victoria whose **Balmoral Castle** is the epitome of the 19th-century Scottish castellated mansion.

These *baronial* mansions are outwith the scope of this book, but it is as well to recognise the source of their design, derived from the

OPPOSITE: *West Lodge, Scoulag, Mountstuart, Bute. Robert Weir Schultz, 1895–1896. Though generous for a gate-lodge, this is not a big house, yet the steeply pitched roof and central chimney stack convey the verticality of the tower-house (Historic Scotand).*

tower-house, which in turn drew on the earlier defensive castle. Bartizans, crowsteps, decorated dormers, tall chimney stacks, features that are all associated with the Scottish castellated tradition. These were adapted to adorn large houses, helping their owners to feel part of the establishment, to give a sense of inheritance. The accommodation was, of course very different from either the castle or the tower-house, often with grand entrance, impressive main staircase, suites of rooms and vast kitchen and service quarters besides extensive housing for staff.

Kirkton Cottages, Fortingall, 1889, James Marjoribanks Maclaren; combination of English and Scots vernacular revival in Perthshire: crowsteps, eyebrow dormers, English type thatch (Historic Scotland).

The grandiose baronial gave way to a quieter style, drawn from Scottish architectural tradition but used less flamboyantly, influenced by the **Arts and Crafts** movement led in England by William Morris, with its ethos of truth to original materials and form coupled with a new recognition of the vernacular. From this grew the awareness of building tradition as a design source. The domestic tower-house, the lairds' house and even the cottage provided inspiration, suggesting local masonry or quiet harled walls, crowsteps, dormers, nepus gables and sometimes modest bartizans for middle class houses in country and suburbs or adaptation of earlier buildings for more comfortable and spacious living. Where there was restoration of an original building, this respected, as far as was practicable, the original fabric.

In Scotland **Robert Lorimer** was the doyenne of this movement but there were others such as John Kinross, Frank Deas, W L Carruthers (Inverness). Lorimer restored with sympathy for the earlier fabric: **Balmanno**, Perthshire is a rescued, harled L-plan tower-house, while **Dunderave**, Argyll rises five storeys high, an original tower-house with sympathetic additions in similar stonework. Lorimer also designed new houses, always relating these fine Edwardian homes to the local landscape and the Scottish vernacular tradition from which their inspiration was drawn. John Kinross (1855–1931) designed mansions and churches, besides smaller estate buildings based on traditional themes with exquisite attention to detail. At Fortingal, Perthshire, John Marjoribanks MacLaren (1843–1890) designed a series of estate cottages drawing on both English Arts and Crafts and Scottish vernacular themes.

Yet concurrently with its revival the indigenous vernacular cottage and house was being built in the Highlands and Islands until the turn of the 1900s, and lived in, in some cases with little modernisation, until recently. Over the years slate, pantiles or felt roofs have replaced most thatch. Changing practices in fishing have meant that many fishermen, while keeping their homes in their village of origin, no longer use these homes as the work place. Many of these fishertowns are congested, leaving little room for cottage enlargement so the additional space provided by the empty gear store is welcomed for home improvements such as the installation of modern bathrooms and flush sanitation.

In country areas the ubiquitous bungalow replaces many an *auld hoose*, which in turn is given over to stock, hens, adapted as a garage or used for storage. In others accommodation has been increased

Kellas House, Moray, Frank Deas, 1914. Scots revival: harled with warm brown/grey Caithness slate roof, tall chimney stacks, stair turret projecting from angle and terminating with a conical roof. This architectural vocabulary is from tower-houses and merchant dwellings and looks very much at home in this just post-Edwardian era country house (Beaton).

with extensions; dormers eke out roof space – some in sympathetic scale, others as precariously-perched oversize boxes. Depopulation of isolated rural areas sadly leaves empty ruins, roofless where thatching has rotted away but reasonably sound if slate was the original covering. The vernacular cottage is fragile.

During the past quarter century there has been a surge of tower-house restoration; often roofless and ruined, they have found sympathetic and brave new owners who have discovered the satisfaction and excitement of restoration besides creating a special home.

Small vernacular cottages do not always adapt easily to modern living: the survival of some regional examples has been ensured as museums for locals and visitors. There is also simple reuse for tourists. In the Western Isles some abandoned blackhouses serve as hostels for back-packing tourists, jointly administered by the Gatliff Hebridean Hostels Trust and the Scottish Youth Hostels Association. The same type of reuse has been initiated by the Shetland Amenity Trust which has adapted a variety of buildings in Shetland as *camping böds*, something on the lines of *stone tents* in the north of England where obsolete field barns offer overnight accommodation to walkers.

The introduction of *statutory listing* under the 1972 Town and Country Planning (Scotland) Act gives protection to and identifies buildings of vernacular interest as well as famous castles and the works of great architects. *Listing* makes for supervisory control over alterations of *listed* buildings: the procedure can also facilitate grant aid.

The Scottish Vernacular Buildings Working Group, established in 1972, draws together those interested in Scotland's traditional buildings, tower-house and tollhouse, croft and cottage, fishertown and farm. Membership is open to all, there are visits, conferences and an annual journal. It is these people and groups who draw attention to the rich variety of Scotland's traditional buildings. . . which is also the purpose of this book.

*Helmsdale, Sutherland
(George Tuckwell)*

GLOSSARY

Ashlar: smooth polished building stone with narrow courses, mainly facework

Architraves: see jambs

Astragal(s): window glazing bar(s)

Bandcourse: horizontal masonry band carried across the face of a building, similar to the stringcourse but flat

Bartizan: battlemented or conical-roofed angle turret

Bellcast: a light flattening of the roof near the eaves to throw rainwater away from a wallface

Cherry-caulking: (*cherry-cocking*): infilling random rubble with small stones to make regular masonry courses

Cherry-pointing: (Angl. *galleting*): stone fragments inserted in mortar while still soft to level courses; structural and ornamental

Corbelling: jutting or projecting of stonework, in progressive courses producing inward curving profile

Creel-house: cruck-and wattle-framed house clad with turf sods.

Crowstep: stepped gable

Draw-bar: a solid wooden bar drawn across the inside of a door to prevent opening; housed in a mural slot (a slot within the wall) when not in use

Fenestration: arrangement of windows in a building

Galleting: see cherry-caulking

Gun-loop: access hole through wall for directing fire

Hanging lum: wide wooden hearth canopy, directly over the open fire, drawing smoke upwards in a tapering flue projecting above the roof as a chimney

Harl: roughcast, a lime and grit mix serving as a waterproof coating

Jamb(s): side(s) of a door or window opening

Margin: sides, lintel and often sill edge of window or door opening, sometimes painted

Nepus gable: small usually cenred gable carried up from the top of a wall with a dormer-like roof and usually a window

Piended: *Scots* : hipped

Rubble: shapeless stones, either coursed or uncoursed (random rubble)

Scale and platt stairs: stairs consisting of straight flights of steps with mezzanine landing, all flights abutting either side of a central masonry spine wall

Skew: flat coping to gable

Skewputt: lower stone of gable coping, usually projecting and moulded, sometimes with armorial, date or initials of original owner

Stringcourse: horizontal line of projecting stone moulding carried along face of building: see also bandcourse

Timpan gable: *see* Nepus gable

Tower-house: vertical castellated dwelling

Wheel-stair (also turnpike): narrow spiral stair, usually stone

Yett: *Scots* : heavy iron grill gate with interwoven bars; normally inside main door of tower-house

References

CHAPTER 1

Clifton-Taylor, Alec, *The Pattern of English Building* (1972), pp. 10, 33. *Imperial Gazetteer of Scotland* ii (c. 1858-60), p. 496.

CHAPTERS 1 AND 7

Love, John, and McMullen, Brenda (Eds), *A Salmon for the Schoolhouse: A Nairnshire parish in the nineteenth century from the diaries of Robert and Elsie Thomson* (1994), p. 10.

CHAPTER 3

Sage, Donald, *Memorabilia Domestica* (1889), p. 5.

INDEX

FURTHER READING

Two series of generously illustrated Scottish architectural guides are aimed at the general reader. Firstly *Exploring Scotland's Heritage* (The Stationery Office and Royal Commission on the Ancient and Historical Monuments of Scotland) edited by Anna Ritchie, recently revised and re-issued 1992−7, and secondly *Illustrated Architectural Guides* published by the Rutland Press for the Royal Incorporation of Architects in Scotland.

Other useful books include: John G Dunbar, *The Architecture of Scotland* (1978); Robert J Naismith, *Buildings of the Scottish Countryside* (1985); Nigel Tranter, *The Fortified House in Scotland,* vols *i-v* (1962-70, new ed., 1977); Alexander Fenton and Bruce Walker, *The Rural Architecture of Scotland* (1981) and Annette Carruthers (Ed.), *The Scottish Home* (1996). For industrial housing and tollhouses, John R Hume, *The Industrial Archaeology of Scotland* vol i, (1976), vol ii (1977), and for gate-lodges, Tim Mowl and Brian Earnshaw, *Trumpet at a Distant Gate* (1985). The Scottish Vernacular Buildings Working Group focus on building traditions producing an annual journal, *Vernacular Building,* and occasional publications.

SELECTIVE LIST OF SITES TO VISIT

Chapter 2

Broch of Gurness, Orkney (Historic Scotland)
Brough of Birsay, Orkney (Historic Scotland)
Dun Carloway, Lewis, Western Isles (Historic Scotland)
Glenelg Brochs, Lochalsh, Inverness-shire (Historic Scotland)
Jarlshof, Shetland (Historic Scotland)
Knap of Howar, Papa Westray, Orkney (Historic Scotland)
Mousa Broch, Shetland (Historic Scotland)
Skara Brae, Orkney (Historic Scotland)

Chapter 3

42 Arnol, Lewis, Western Isles (Historic Scotland)
Auchindrain (joint tenancy farm), Inveraray, Argyll
Corrigal Farm Museum, Harray, Orkney
Kirbister, Orkney
Crofthouse Museum, Voe, Shetland
Colbost Cottage Museum, Dunvegan, Skye
Luib Folk Museum, near Broadford, Skye
Highland Folk Museum, Kingussie, Inverness-shire
Laidhay, Dunbeath, Caithness
Moirlanich Longhouse, Killin, Perthshire (National Trust for Scotland)
Scottish Agricultural Museum, Ingliston, Edinburgh
Skye Museum of Island Life, Kilmuir

Chapter 4

Castle of Park, Kirkcudbrightshire (Historic Scotland)
Claypotts, Dundee (Historic Scotland)
Culross, Fife, The Palace and The Study, (National Trust for Scotland)
Greenknowe Tower, Berwickshire (Historic Scotland)
Huntingtower Castle, Perth (Historic Scotland)
Kellie Castle, Fife (National Trust for Scotland)
MacLellan's Castle, Kirkcudbright (Historic Scotland)
Muness Castle, Shetland (Historic Scotland)
Scalloway, Shetland (Historic Scotland)

Scotstarvit Tower (Historic Scotland)
Smailholm Tower (Historic Scotland)

Chapters 5 & 6

Gladstones's Land, Lawnmarket, Edinburgh (National Trust for Scotland)
Culross, Fife (National Trust for Scotland)
Provost Ross's House, Shiprow, Aberdeen (Aberdeen Maritime Museum)
Tankerness House, Kirkwall, Orkney (Kirkwall Museum)
The Batchelors' Club, Tarbolton, Ayrshire (National Trust for Scotland)
Thomas Carlyle's birthplace, Ecclefechan, Dumfriesshire (National Trust for Scotland)

Chapter 7

Angus Folk Museum, Glamis, Angus (National Trust for Scotland)
Barrie's birth place, Kirriemuir, Angus
Kinnaird Head Lighthouse, Fraserburgh, Aberdeenshire (Historic Scotland)
New Lanark, planned town
Signal Tower Museum, Arbroath, Angus (Angus Council)
Souter Johnnie's Cottage, Kirkoswald, Ayrshire (National Trust for Scotland)
Wanlockhead lead mines, visitors' trail
Weaver's Cottage, Kilbarchan, Renfrewshire (National Trust for Scotland)

Chapter 8

Anstruther Fisheries Museum, Fife
Wick Heritage Museum, Wick, Caithness
Signal Tower Museum, Arbroath, Angus
Maggie's Hoosie, Inverallochy, near Fraserburgh, Aberdeenshire
The Buckie Drifter, Buckie, Banffshire
Tugnet Icehouse Museum, Tugnet, Moray

Printed in Scotland for The Stationery Office Limited
by CC No. 56901 30C 6/97.